LOVIN' LIFE ...

A COLLECTION OF HUMOR COLUMNS

by **MAC LANE**

D1569133

For Lacern

CONTENTS

I'm the Man of Her Dreams

———•••———

My wife woke up furious with me.

Instead of the usual kiss, I got a furrowed brow and a toxic glare before she marched off into the bathroom.

Oh boy, I thought. What have I done now?

I have a powerful ability, perfected by 12 years of marriage, to hack my wife off…beyond belief.

My power is so awesome at times, I can have her Bobby-Knight-on-a-losing-streak mad without seemingly any effort at all.

Think Mac.

My mind was quickly cataloging our conversion from the previous night. My mental rolodex spinning, trying to recall any remark that may have come out the wrong way, or that could have been potentially misunderstood, that would cause her to act like this. When I'm in the doghouse, I usually know why, but this morning was different.

Stumped, I peeked into the bathroom where Angry Wife brushed her teeth with a venomous expression.

"Good morning Merry Sunshine," I said with a big toothy grin that I hoped conveyed –I'm not at all mad at you but I can see that you are mighty put out with me.

"Why are you so mad?" I ventured.

"Last night, I needed your help and you wouldn't help me," she said.

"Was one of the kids throwing up?" I asked, knowing that I've slept through such episodes before. Not to say I'm a heavy sleeper, but once a car crashed into a tree in the front yard, the police came –light, sirens, and all. I didn't stir.

"No," she said.

"Were you up during the night?" I asked, still clueless.

"No, in my dream," she explained. "I was being chased off a cliff....I was hang-ing there. I was scared and needed you. I called to you for help, and you said –in your ugliest tone of voice– that wouldn't help me. Then you walked away, just when I needed you most."

"Wait a minute. You woke up mad at me because of something you dreamed?" I asked.

"You wouldn't help me. You were mean and ugly."

"Oh." I said dumbstruck. "Let me get this straight, you are not mad at me because of anything I actually did. You are mad at me because of something I did in your dream?"

Honestly, I didn't know whether to feel relieved or not, nor did I know how to respond. On the one hand, I could have chosen to stand my ground. I had a pretty good case. I was sure I could convincingly argue that while she had every right to be furious at me in dream-world, I didn't actually do anything wrong –I mean in awake-world– so you can't carry a grudge over from one world to the other. Right?

Or I could just apologize. It was obvious she was upset and needed reassurance that I wasn't the bad guy of her nightmare.

"I'm sorry," I said, feeling like a tremendous weenie for apologizing for some-thing she dreamed I did. But, what the heck, isn't that what being married is all about?

She apologized too and gave me a hug.

In bed the next night, I gave her a little pat as she started to doze off.

"I love you," she said.

"I love you too," I said as I looked at her.

She is the woman of my dreams, I thought. So what, if I'm not the man of her dreams in her dreams. I'm pretty sure I am in real life.

Getting Professional Help

———•••———

My marriage needs professional help.

We've been trying for years to decorate our house.

My wife has good taste; I think I have good taste, but the trouble starts when our good tastes collide.

She wanted the kitchen repainted in a terra-cotta color, where as I preferred frond green. Both are attractive colors, to be sure. So which did we choose?

We didn't.

Since I'm a salesman by trade, I tried to sell her on my color. I marched around the kitchen waving a copy of Southern Living; gesturing at the walls with sweeping motions of my hand –like Bob Barker's beauties revealing the grand showcase prize. I urged her, implored her, beseeched her to just try and imagine how terrific frond green kitchen walls will look. If only she would say YES.

Since my wife is a mom by trade, she has no problem saying NO. She folded her arms, and shook her head during my theatrics. She waited until I finished, paused and said, "I don't like it."

Like Gilligan and the gang, who every week hatched a different scheme to get off the island, I also kept trying –without success– to change her mind. I tried to rally support among our children by coaching them to cheer and clap –like holding a mini pep rally for my green color chip.

Dirty sneak attacks like this just served to make her even more resolved. As a mother of three –she's used to being outnumbered.

Secretly, I think she wishes I would just stay out of the decorating entirely. I suspect she wants me to be like a Ward Cleaver sort of guy who takes his pipe

3

from his mouth, furrows his brow and says, "I think the terra-cotta would look just great dear," as he pecks her on the cheek.

I, on the other hand, see myself as a modern diaper changing sort of man, the sort of man who will get up at 3:00 AM to tend to a sick child, the sort of man who does dishes, and yes, the sort of man that has strong feelings about wall color.

At a stalemate, we ended up leaving the room painted the same old color –a sickening shade of burgundy that was trendy in the Reagan administration. Ironically, we agree on this color. We both hate it.

About a year and a half ago, we embarked on our most ambitious project yet, we added-on to the house. Since my wife and I can't reach an agreement on even a picture frame, we decided that we needed professional help.

We called in Alan Ferguson and Associates. Alan and his design partner, John Paulin, have proven to be worth their weight in silk draperies. They have done a great job on the house. They drew up the floor plan for the addition and worked with the builders every step of the way. We both loved everything they picked out and –as an added benefit of their services– we don't fight about wall color anymore.

This new arrangement has, however, created a new problem. We love everything Alan and John do so much; we want more -lots' more- but we don't have nearly the budget to do it all. Forced to be selective, now we fight about which room to decorate next. "The kitchen," she says. "No, the office," I say and so it goes.

To help out with the decorating expenses, I've tried to earn some extra money on the side by writing this column.

So far, my writing has earned about enough to pay for half a throw pillow. But with Alan and John picking it out it will be the prettiest half throw pillow anywhere around.

At least we can both agree on that.

Orange Juice Wars

———•••———

I zig. I zag. And I backtrack across the store.

I go up and down aisles sometimes four and five times.

I can't tell you how many times I've ordered say, cold cuts, at the deli counter and forgotten to pick them up until I'm deep into the check-out line, or on one particularly frustrating occasion, in my driveway.

In short, I'm not very good at shopping for groceries.

I was in the store the other day, doing my best to check off the items on my list –Lettuce– check. Ketchup– check. Salad Dressing –check. I thought I was doing pretty well until I reached the Orange Juice section.

I just stood there, mouth agape. I had no idea.

Until this minute, I had naively assumed that orange juice was just orange juice. I was quite unprepared for the multitude of choices I saw before me: Original No Pulp, Original Home-Style Some Pulp, Original Grove Stand Lots of Pulp. Never in my life, before this very instant, had I ever considered what level of pulp I prefer in my O.J.

In addition to the pulp factor the major brands, Minute Made and Tropicana, were offering: Added Calcium with Vitamin D No Pulp, Healthy Kids with added Vitamins A, C, E and Calcium, Heart Wise, and Home Squeezed Style. Apparently, the only variety they don't offer is: Just Pulp with No Juice.

I remember the "Burger Wars" from some years back with Burger King, McDonald's, and Wendy's slugging it out, each trying to outdo the other with new ads and new products: "Where's the beef?" and all that. Now, as I stood there next to my shopping cart scratching my head, I felt as if I had unwittingly stepped onto the battlefield of some sinister Orange Juice War.

There were so many choices. I thought: This is worse than ordering at Starbucks.

I had to pick one, but which one? Calcium is good for the kids, right? But is it better than Immunity Defense or the one called Healthy Kids with all the added vitamins and stuff? Maybe I could get the Heart Healthy for me and to heck with the kids? Nah. The Home Squeezed one has a nice sound, but apparently it doesn't offer all the other healthy goodies.

The longer I stood there reading the various O.J. labels the more frustrated I became.

Finally, and maybe by default, I lifted the Donald Duck brand from the shelf and placed it into my buggy. I can't remember having ever tasted Donald Duck's orange juice before, but I was relieved by the fact Mr. Duck made no claims about his juice. He didn't ask me to decide what level of pulpiness I desired or what vitamins were the most vital. Donald's label was also refreshingly simple. It read "Orange Juice" and nothing else, and it was the nothing else part that appealed to me the most.

Plus, I must admit, I felt a bit smug, thinking maybe, I had outsmarted the marketing and strategy geniuses that the big brands employ.

When I got home my wife asked, "Why on earth did you buy Donald Duck Orange Juice?" in the same tone of voice I imagine she might use if I had brought home a bag of Cruella De'vil Puppy Chow....or a box of Captain Hook Fabric Softener.

She went on to inform me that we only buy Tropicana Added Calcium with Vitamin D No Pulp.

Think of me as the Orange Juice War's first casualty.

Over-Scheduled and Over-Tired

————•••————

I remember Saturdays when I was a kid.

We'd hang out at home, Dad and I washing the car perhaps. After we finished, Dad would ask –in his Ray Steven's voice, "How 'bout a cold drink Ethel?" He didn't really call me Ethel; he just liked to parody the song about "streaking" that was popular at the time.

"Sure," I'd say, and we drove to the 7-11.

I remember that was a big deal –an outing– driving with Dad to get a Coke. More than likely, this was the only time we left the house all day.

Saturday, for the Modern-Day Lanes, usually starts off with Anna, our youngest, waking at 5:00am sharp. My wife and I will try to coax her back to sleep. Our attempts at coaxing her into renewed slumber usually fail, forcing one of us to get up with her. Anna and I have enjoyed many sunrises together.

The other two kids and my wife, Michele, will wake between 7:00 and 8:00 whereupon the five of us get showered, dressed and fed.

Grabbing coolers, snacks, folding chairs, cleats, balls, birthday gifts, bathing suits for swim practice and sometimes Madison, our dog, we pile out of the house with as much equipment as a team of Sherpas preparing for an Everest assault.

Who has to be where when? Michele and I were up the night before, planning our strategy for the approaching day.

On your mark. Get set. Go. As we charge to a birthday party our youngest has been invited to attend, a family reunion in Burlington, a soccer game for my oldest in Winston, Anna's nap (preferably but not always at home), a birthday party for my brother-in-law in Charlotte, and another local party that same evening.

Oh, and I almost forgot, a cook-out banquet for the soccer team Saturday night as well.

I'm not making this up. This is our actual itinerary for Oct. 25th. Saturdays are always hectic, some a little less, some a little more, but this routine is fairly typical. At the end of a day like this, I regret to say, Michele and I are both so tired that we are less than patient with the whiny complaints of the children –good kids– who are really just as weary as we are.

Hopefully, my girls are not going to look back and discover their childhood was spent inside a minivan. They might reminisce about Chick fil-As, bought on the go, as we raced to make another event.

Our youngest, poor Anna, has been strapped, harnessed and buckled into a car seat more times than Richard Petty and she's only two.

The lazy weekends –that I enjoyed as a kid– don't exist for the contemporary Lanes. My girls may never know the peaceful pleasure of a Saturday afternoon with nothing to do.

Michele and I agree that we are constantly over-booked and aware that it's become a problem.

We need to get our calendars out and find a solution to this over-scheduling dilemma. We should pick a Saturday in mid-February that looks good and jointly schedule a time to have a family-wide, lazy Saturday afternoon. Maybe we could shoot for between 4:30 and 5:00pm –in between the soccer match and the sleepover.

Seriously, my life was full growing-up, even though it was filled with less activity. Dad and I had the time to shoot baskets, wash the car or go for a "cold drink Ethel" on Saturday afternoons.

I've started to realize that less stuff on the calendar can actually mean more – much more in the life of a child.

Good at Not Finding Things

———•••———

I was rooting around in the cupboard Saturday –down on the bottom shelf where the dishtowels and placemats are kept –when a strange thing happened.

I discovered my wife's secret stash. It seems that Michele Lane, my bride of 19 years, had secretly hidden one of those seriously large Costco-size bags of M&M's chocolate candy underneath the placemats.

Never one to pass up an opportunity to have a little fun, I decided to confront her with my finding.

"Ahhhh Haaaa," I said, "Look what I found!" as I held the bag up for inspection. I shook it up and down a bit to demonstrate that it was about 3/4 of the way empty, as I grinned a big "gotcha" smile for emphasis.

I don't know what sort of reaction I was expecting: a little embarrassment maybe? A tad bit of good natured annoyance perhaps?

I definitely did not expect her jaw to drop nearly to the floor with a look of complete shock and total disbelief.

If I had pulled a live chimpanzee out from the cupboard, I don't think I would have rocked her world this badly.

She held her finger up, furrowed her brows and spoke softly, but in a deadly serious, tone of voice, "I want to know….I want to know…. how on earth you found those M&M's?"

I shrugged, and was about to say something about how I was simply looking for the placemats, when she cut me off.

"You can't find anything." She said getting louder, "You don't know where the Band-Aids are. You don't know where the envelopes are. You can't find the tape measure. You don't know where the thermometer is. You use the good guest towels to wash the car because you can't...," she made these little quotation gesture with her fingers "....find the car-wash towels. You wear brand new pants outside to mow the grass, and you come back in with oil and grass stains all over them because you claim..." little air-quotes again, "...not to be able to find you old ones."

I couldn't argue.

She was 100% correct on every count.

I admit it. I spend hours every week just looking for (and not finding) things.

And it seems to be getting worse as I get older. Sometimes I'll start out looking for a pair of scissors for example, and find myself staring blankly into the cabinet over the washing machine and wondering, "What the heck am I doing here? And what the heck am I looking for?"

I also have a bad habit of improvising if I can't find something.

The other day I couldn't find my hammer, so I used the flat end of the hedge clippers to drive in a few loose nails on my fence.

I can only imagine what my neighbors must think: "There goes Mac with the hedge clippers, wonder what he's going to hammer this time?"

My wife's outburst went on for several minutes and concluded with: "...so I just want to know how you able to find my secret bag of M&M's, when you can't seem to find anything else in this whole entire house?"

In the days since this happened, I've given that question a lot of thought.

And, truthfully, I haven't been able to find a good answer to that either.

Wine

——•••——

A few years ago I could not have told you the difference between Merlot and Mercurochrome. Or Chardonnay and Calamine for that matter.

I guess you could say that I was a bit of a wine bumpkin.

But thanks to my father-in-law, I have a newly discovered appreciation for wine, particularly red wines. I enjoy them. But I'm still a little conflicted on this whole wine business.

Conflicted because, I don't totally understand wine, and if the truth be known, I don't see how anyone can understand wine. The following is from a wine review I read recently (I'm not making this up): "…unfined, unfiltered, explosively-scented, richly-textured, a full-bodied red. Made from Syrah, it offers big, smoky, earthy scents intermixed with notions of saddle leather, licorice, copious blackberry as well as cassis fruit with a slight mid-palate of lead pencil."

When I read this type of description, the more romantic side of me gets carried away. I imagine myself sitting with other sophisticated wine tasters with palates so refined as to be able to discern the subtlest hints of cassis fruit in each glorious vintage we sample and carrying on lively conversations in this fashion. I imagine that I am the sort of fellow who can look the wine guy –who's actually called a sommelier– but I didn't know that until I just looked it up –straight in the eye and, without the slightest hesitation, order a bottle of Guigal Chateauneuf-du-Pape, pronouncing it properly, with the confidence of an old pro.

In real life however, and this is where the bumpkin shows itself, I am more likely to wonder: Where exactly is the mid-palate? Why saddle leather? Why not glove leather or Bomber-jacket leather or even ostrich leather? And why lead pencil? Why not a hint of sidewalk chalk? Or Sharpie? I would never expect any of these things to be lurking around in my glass.

Also, I can't help but wonder who writes all this stuff? It's as if the only goal is to make the wine sound old, and romantic rather than to describe what it actually tastes like. In this light, I guess I can see why saddle leather works and shoe leather clearly would not.

So you see what I mean about being conflicted? Half of me really wants to buy into this whole sophisticated stuff, while the other half of me still wonders how anyone can possibly believe that a sip of fermented grape juice can actually generate such seemingly endless description.

Next, and this may be even more confusing, is this whole business of region one must deal with to become an expert in wines. This is new to me because, my former beverage of choice was Budweiser, and after all, nobody really cares where beer comes from.

Here is an example I read, "Origin- Paso Robles, San Luis Obispo, Central Coast, California, USA." I got out my map and looked up exactly where this place is.

The town of St. Luis Obispo, California, is actually on Highway 101, about 120 miles northwest of Los Angeles, just north of Vandenberg Air Force base. I agree that Central Coast, California, does have an exotic ring to it, and "Just up from the Air Force base," or "Just off Highway 101" might cause one to think the wine may contain an explosively scented notion of jet fuel or diesel exhaust amid the other earthy scents and might best be left off the label as the intent is not for you to actually find the place, or even to necessarily know where it is. Rather, it's more to romanticize their product in the same way that bottled water brands always seem to tout the fact that they originate from some place mountainous, cold and springy.

Anyway, I'm still just learning about wine and for the moment I'll just have to do the best I can.

At least I have learned enough so far not to order a bottle of '96 Mercurochrome, unless I cut myself at the table.

Children's Names

———•••———

Apparently, Lisa & David are not fashionable. Tom & Jill are archaic. Michael & Jennifer –who were once the epitome of chic– are now as outdated as rotary dial.

I made this observation walking in my daughter's elementary school. The hallways are festooned with children's art this time of year and what I noticed was not the artwork itself; rather the names of the students affixed to each project. The names read: Garrick, Lena, Brianna, Askia, Morgan and Wavy.

My interest now peaked, I started paying attention to this new crop of children's names all over town. What I have learned is, and my apologies to grandma and grandpa, but there is not one single: Ida, Agnes, Trudy, Elmo, Claude, Elijah, Evelyn, Eula, Myrtle, Elbert, Harold, Howard, June, Ralph, Frank, or Homer in my daughter's whole school. The names from your generation have fallen by the wayside, right along with the Jeff and Jennifers from mine.

Sorry Charlie. Sorry Julie. Your solid American sounding names, are giving way to the stylish. The trend nowadays is to appoint children with distinctive and imaginative tags. Some of these new names come from nature like Summer, Ocean, Storm, Rivers, Autumn, Jasmine and Amber or from places like Savannah, Austin, Dallas, Chyna, Charlotte and Brooklyn.

Some new names are really old-fashioned names that have an air of sophistication like Sophia, Gabriella, and for boys Jackson. Kate and Kaitlyn is another one: Our Indian Princess tribe has 12 girls and 1/3 of them are named Kate or Katie, no kidding.

Presidential sounding names are also wildly popular. You can't be around children very long without bumping into at least three or four kids named Madison, one or two named Jackson, Kennedy, and Reagan.

I identify with the imaginatively named child, as I was known as MacArthur for my early years and later shortened it to Mac. Growing up, there were usually always 2 Jeffs and 3 Johns in my classes, but I was always the only Mac and I liked it that way.

Being a Mac also has its problems. It sounds too much like the more common: Matt, Mark, Max, and Mike. So when I'm introduced I usually end up saying, "Ah No. Actually it's Mac, M-a-c." I will sometimes add helpfully, " like the Big Mac hamburger." Also, I will admit that I sometimes get tired of correcting and just roll with it letting the person call me Mark or Matt, particularly if the chances are slim that I'll ever see the person again in my lifetime.

I can't really fault people who miss-hear my name. Mac sounds common enough, but there really are not many of us. In my 36 years, I have met hundreds of Marks, and even more Johns, Mikes and Steves, but the Macs are rare.

The other day, I was talking to a friend with a daughter named Hannah. He said, "When we named our daughter, we thought we were being so novel and original. Now, there are 2 other Hannahs in her class."

With unusual names becoming so common place, if you want to name your kids something really unusual, you might want to consider a name like Mary or Dick to really be different.

The Wall

——•••——

We weren't prepared for the wall.

We posed for pictures in front of F.D.R. We chanced upon Miss USA at the Jefferson. We decided not to wait in the two-hour line at the Washington Monument on that sweaty, summer weekend in D.C.

We were having a great time and, I must admit, I felt like Clark Griswald, in "National Lampoon's Vacation," as I spouted on about notable historical facts. The kids only rolled their eyes a few times, as I explained that was the very spot that Martin Luther King gave his famous "Dream Speech."

At 9 and 6, my girls were a little young for this sort of lesson but I couldn't help it; I am a history nut and the kids seemed to be tolerating me admirably.

Make a quick stop at the Vietnam Memorial, then grab a bite to eat.

"You know kids, your Daddy Mason fought in Vietnam," I said, referring to my stepfather, in an effort to add interest.

As we walked along the path, the black granite wall gradually grew in height from only a few inches to an altitude requiring a ladder to reach the top. On every inch were names engraved in the onyx stone. Without realizing it, we had all stopped our conversation. The other tourists had also ceased talking –a sensation like walking into a cathedral, only outdoors.

We stopped and just stared. We were staring at the names, thousands of names. Panel after panel. Name after name. Goose bumps erupted on my arms. "I had no idea," I said, as if offering a prayer. "There are so many names."

Decorations of handwritten notes, flowers, and scattered pictures, served as touching remembrances that humanized the stone.

1967, I am a generation removed from Vietnam. I'm not old
have known anyone who is listed on the wall, so I pointed to one name
om and read it aloud, "You see this name here, Charles Edwin Bray, Jr."
children nodded.

"He had a mother who loved him," I said. "A father, maybe even a brother or a sister who loved him too. I'll bet he had a girlfriend and he might have wanted to get married someday. Maybe he dreamed of becoming a dad himself, taking his family on vacation. But none of those things happened, because he died. He died in a far-away country called Vietnam and all that's left of him are the memories of those who knew him and this name on the wall."

Close to tears now, I gestured to the wall, "Each one of those names represents a boy –or in a few cases, a girl– who had a mother that loved them and who had hopes and dreams about growing up and growing old."

"Can we touch it?" my daughter asked.

As we stood there in the sweltering heat, we touched the wall, but more importantly, the wall touched us.

It's Fall

————•••————

It's fall and fall means football.

I love football…..or at least I used to.

Last year, I went to see the Maryland-UNC game. If you happened to catch the game, my beloved Tar Heels matched up with the Terps about as well as a Bradford pear tree matches up to an ice storm. The Carolina team found themselves –like the tree– completely covered, bending backwards at odd angles against the weight of a superior force. Maryland piled up points like broken branches piling up on the ground.

Midway through the third quarter, we left the game. We just couldn't take it anymore. Incidentally, Kenan Stadium is the only ball-field I know of where, if you want to escape the traffic when you leave, it's best to stay for the entire game. The exodus of disheartened fans begins at half-time and continues on into the 3rd quarter, and by the 4th quarter, there is waaaaay more Carolina blue on I- 40 than in the stadium seats.

The game was the worst at home defeat since the 1920's. The final score was Maryland-59 UNC-7.

My other team, the Carolina Panthers, have staggered like a drunk at closing time through the last two seasons, losing 24 times, while winning only 8 games.

Collectively, the Tar Heels and the Panthers lost twice for each time they won once. The teams have a combined record of 38 losses to just 19 wins over the last two seasons.

My excitement for the sport of football has taken a beating like the teams I love.

Please don't think that I'm one of those pouty-pants-football-fans who walks around the office with his lower lip pooched out with every defeat. (I used to be that guy, but my lips got tired from so much pooching.) I think all UNC fans have done some serious pooching over the years.

Is it too much to ask that maybe one of these two teams could be at least competitive? I'm realistic enough not to dream of National Championships or Super Bowls; I'd settle for competitive, or competent, maybe even not-embarrassing.

I'm just about to the point where I really don't care about football anymore. The season has barely even begun and I feel like I already know the outcome of the games –my teams lose.

I feel about football the way Muhammad Ali must have felt after his last fight with Spinks; face bruised and eyes swollen with that vacant stare. I'm finding myself unable to get back in the ring again to face another pounding this season.

This fall, I think I'm going to take the money I usually spend on games and do something more exciting with it –like buy cow manure for the garden.

Sorry football, you'll have to manage without me this season; I'm going to sit this one out.

By the way, if UNC can somehow beat Florida State this Saturday, if Carolina can somehow miraculously manages a win, I'll take back everything I just said.

Naaah, it'll never happen.

Note: In the 2003 season opener, UNC politely lost to Florida State by a score of 37-0, and would go on to a 2 win and 10 loss season. The Panthers, however, would finish 11-5 and win their division, the NFC Championship, and appear in the Super Bowl for the first time.

Olympic Napping

———•••———

If napping were an Olympic sport, I think I could compete at a pretty high level.

I imagine Bob Costas and Marv Albert with the commentary: "Ya know Marv, I watched Lane in the qualifying round. He nailed his routine. Nearly the instant his head hit the pillow, he started to snore and when I say snore I mean really snore. His snorts and snuffles could rival even the legendary Shep from the Three Stooges."

"Your right Bob, there's nobody better at snoring than Lane, but his overall style is what impressed the judges the most. He isn't known for his cute-cuddly-teddy-bear approach like many other competitive sleepers, instead of dozing peacefully and innocently, Lane looks as if he may require medical attention at any moment. His arms fall from his chest and hang over the bedside with knuckles brushing the floor, and every now and then he has a series of spasms where his entire body seems to twitch and vibrate as if he were being touched on the rear-end by an electric cattle prod."

"He really has been at the top of his game for some time now, and he's one of the most energetic sleepers in the whole competition."

"Wait. Here comes Lane onto the floor in his team USA nightshirt, taking his position next to the bed."

"Well, it all comes down to this, the final round, for the gold."

"The teams from Mexico have dominated for years and this Olympics is no exception. Pedro Noche-Siesta, of Mexico, is in the lead with a score of 9.8, followed by the Russian, Yawn Hibernateski, with a 9.75. These are the scores that Lane has to beat."

"Lane enters the bed. His first move should be the cool-side-pillow-flip, but the judges declared, just hours before the competition, that this move would not be graded as highly as previously thought. So, let's see what Lane has come up with here."

"Oh wow! It's the over-the-head-reach-and-grab-an-extra-pillow-from-the-wife's-side-of the-bed move. It's flawless! Look at his follow-through, notice how he gently tucks the extra pillow between his knees. Oh, my. I think he's going to score high marks for that one."

"Good volume on the snore Marv, it sounds like a locomotive with a head cold in here. Also, notice how his lips flutter about when he exhales."

"His flappy mouth reminds me of an unzipped tent in a windstorm."

"Marv, I interviewed Lane before the competition and he said that he sometimes imagines himself falling helplessly into a giant hole during the first few minutes of sleep and just before he hits ground, he tightens all his muscles as if bracing for impact."

"Well Bob, that certainly explains the flurry of contorted spasms we just witnessed."

"Look how his mouth hangs agape. There must be several spittoons worth of drool oozing from his mouth onto his pillow and shirt."

"The judges have seen enough. They have awarded Lane the gold medal!"

"Lane is being woken up by his three-year old daughter and trainer, Anna. I'm told when he practices at home for this event, it's usually Anna (or a recorded telephone message urging votes for candidate Dot Kearns) that is primarily responsible for waking him up."

"Mac Lane, bleary eyed, has seen the scores and is just now realizing that he's won the gold!"

"What a great routine Marv."

"I can smell the nap breath from here Bob."

What Do I Do When My Wife Has Got The Flu?

———•••———

When my wife, Michele, came down with the flu,
I thought I would know just what to do.

"How sick do you feel?" I asked her with dread.
"Mac I feel rotten. I can't get out of the bed."

"I've got a fever, a cough, and my throat is sooo sore,
I can't ever remember feeling this crummy before."

"You just lie down," I said, "try to get some rest,
I know what it's like to feel less than your best."

"What about the kids?" Michele asked as she coughed.
"I can't do a thing." She spoke unusually soft.

I knew it was hard for her to lay there infirm,
in the life of mom, there is no time for germs.

"Don't worry about a thing. We can all make do.
I'll just have to do my job, and your job too."

I woke extra early to get the kids ready,
the dishes still dirty from last night's spaghetti.

I got the kids dressed, and packed lunches for eating,
then dashed off to Raleigh for a big business meeting.

I drove back to town to collect the kids from their school,
then raced to the office swearing, "This flu can be cruel."

Quickly, I was learning that when mommy goes down,
the whole house crashes, and problems abound.

Soccer practice, gymnastics, I'm on the run.
The meals don't get cooked, the laundry's undone.

The bills go unpaid; our home life's a shamble,
I think having a sick wife is more than I can handle.

Michele, for her part, was feeling much worse.
if this lasts much longer, she might need a nurse.

Neither of us could stand more of her being sick,
we needed some help and we needed it quick.

So we got on the phone and made a plea for some aid,
S.O.S. we called to the grandparent brigade.

Come Judy, come Charles, come Ann and Daddy Mase.
To our house they all came with a smile on each face.

Like a well trained team, the "grands" knew what to do,
and they all worked together to help beat this rotten flu.

Michele's folks took our youngest -Anna age five.
To keep her a few days or until Michele felt alive.

My mom made ginger ale. She did laundry by the load.
She cooked chicken soup. She even cleaned the commode.

I'm happy to say that with all of the nursing,
my wife is much better, the flu is dispersing.

So to the whole family I say, thanks and thank you,
it was your love that beat a case of "Mom Flu."

Kissing in the Grocery

———•••———

She looked so cute; I just couldn't help myself.

I'm not sure exactly what I was thinking. I didn't really have a plan. I guess you could say that I acted on impulse when I wrapped my arms around my wife Michele and kissed her.

The only problem is that we were standing on aisle five, in front of the salad dressings, in our local grocery store.

Please know that making-out in public isn't something my wife and I do on a regular basis. I won't go so far as to say Michele and I are prudes, but once we leave the privacy of our home, we really aren't a very demonstrative couple.

In fact, it's a rare occurrence for us to even leave the house together without one, two or even all three of the kids along. School, church, sports practices, games…. our lives are so filled with our children, we rarely take the time –or have the energy– to go out just the two of us.

So this may sound a bit pathetic, but a rare trip like this to the grocery –sans kid-dos– felt a little bit like a date to me. (If you've got small children, I'm sure you know what I mean.)

We were chatting about this and that and having a pretty good time picking out groceries. I was enjoying myself and I think Michele was too, and –did I mention how cute she looked?

Like I said, it was an impulse. I hadn't really thought this whole grocery store kissing thing through. Mainly, I hadn't considered what would happen if we got caught?

As we stood there smooching next to the salad dressing, an older woman pushed her cart around the corner and spotted us. She stopped and stared right at Michele and me.

At that instant, I imagined how we must have looked to our spectator: Two forty somethings, who are presumably old enough to know better, necking in a retail establishment.

My wife was the first to realize we had been seen. Had we been nude, I don't think Michele could have been more embarrassed.

Horrified, Michele broke off the kiss, turned to look at the approaching woman, reddened, then gave me a look that seemed to say: Honestly Mac. Did you have to do that right here in the grocery store?

Not wanting our onlooker to get the wrong idea, I blurted out, "We're married." Then, I realized with horror, that what I had just said could make the situation seem worse, much worse, so for clarity I quickly added, "….to each other."

The older lady laughed, smiled and said, "I think it's nice that you two are in love."

And the truth is: I couldn't agree with her more.

Father's Day

———•••———

Before I begin, I just want to wish all the fathers out there, including my own dad, a Happy Father's Day.

In my wildest dreams, I never imagined how great it would be to be a father. I can honestly say that there is nothing, and I mean nothing, in this entire world that I enjoy more than being a dad to my three girls: Carson, Cannon and Anna.

Maybe, this is the reason that I find shopping for a Father's Day card so hard.

I don't know why Father's Day cards are so bad, but they are. They all seem to miss the mark for me.

I know you've seen the ones, those cards with a scene of a father and his young son fishing on a mist covered pond.

Maybe, it's because my special moments as a father cannot be captured by an opaque lens and printed onto glossy card stock. Fatherhood, for me at least, is rarely that neat and tidy.

My special moments as a dad were messy and loud; touching and tear-filled; and once, involved a trip to the hospital.

The first one that leaps to mind was when my, then 5 year old daughter, Anna, broke her arm on a camping trip in the mountains. Holding her hand in the Sparta, NC Emergency Room, I remember how she looked so tiny on that seemingly giant sized stretcher. I also remember the look of fear in her eyes when she asked, "Dad? Will the x-ray hurt?"

"No, no, no," I said. "X-rays don't hurt. X-rays are sort of like getting your picture made." I tried to make my voice sound big and strong for her sake although, I was on the verge of tears myself.

And what happened next would break my heart completely.

The nurse came in and positioned Anna's arm, stepped into the booth. My daughter, in obvious pain, forced herself to smile during the x-ray because she thought she was getting her picture made.

Or when my now 17 year old daughter, went to her first day of kindergarten many years ago. Unable to leave her just yet, my wife and I stood hovering in the doorway. I recall her sitting there at her desk, ringlets of curly hair spilling onto her shoulders and an earnest expression on her face as she mouthed the words, "It's okay. You can go now. I'll be fine." And she has been fine ever since.

Other moments include: Turning Van Halen all the way up while the girls and I cleaned the house. Unstopping toilets. Snaking clogged drains. Driving to Florida while my daughters DJ'd.

So rather than those mass-produced Father's Day cards, I'd much rather get one like I got 8 years ago that was written by my then 6 year old middle daughter (who's now in Driver's Ed). Below is the card written exactly as she wrote it: (note to editor –please print as is)

To: Daddy. I Love You!!!! Love is Love. You ar You. I am mi and i Love you. Love, Love, Love You. I love you Daddy!!! Love Cannon. Daddy. Love you. Cool!!!

This note, actually it was a series of notes written on tiny scraps of paper, was given to me with a pink teddy bear who was wearing a back-pack that my daughter had sewn herself. In the back pack was a band-aid, a cassette tape and a map (in case I get lost) that she had also drawn herself.

The morning she gave it to me, I could tell how proud she was to give me a gift that she had worked so hard to make. This pink teddy bear with his hand sewn back-pack still sits on my desk at work.

This is the kind of Father's Day card that I like. I like the ones that are messy, misspelled and absolutely wonderful.

Youth Soccer: Group Email

——•••——

To: All Lady-Kicker Parents

I want to thank everyone for being sooooooooooo great this year!!! It's not always easy being a working mom and the team's Manager/ Snack Coordinator/ Communication Guru. (You couldn't pay me to do this again!! Kidding!!)

Hopefully, the loss yesterday will be our last!! (Don't even get me started. Dan, you were absolutely correct! Could that referee even see???? The man was impossible! Sorry you got yourself ejected –again.)

Also, I want to give a big Kicker SHOUT OUT!! to Breanna's mom, Becky Smithers, for bringing the cupcakes Saturday! (Did you have to bring soooooooo many? Kidding. My waistline is big enough already!!!!...Kidding.....OK, maybe I'm not kidding?...Kidding!!!)

Moving forward, we have a home game this Saturday at 2:00pm against The Force-Team Gold. Coach Andre says that they were the regional tournament runner-up last year, and they play fast and dirty. I hear they have 2 players in the Pre-Pre-Pre-Olympic Development Program, so this should be a good test for our girls. Go Kickers!!!!

As a reminder, Coach Andre says that playing time will be docked if your player does not attend both the Advanced Skills and Advanced Tactics Training. This is (rain or shine) on Tuesday and Thursday, and this is in addition to the regularly scheduled Mon-Wed-Friday night practices.

For the upcoming fall season, Coach Andre is strongly considering MORNING AND AFTERNOON practices during the week. I know...I know... many of your children attend school. I know this caaaaaaan pose a conflict, for some of you, but I am prepared to go the home school route with Hannah Jane if it will help her to develop and become a better player. We all have to make sacrifices!!!

Come'on people!! We are moving up to the more competitive 8-year old division next year!!!!!!

As we approach the State Tournament, I have been asked to remind all parents (particularly after last week's game….Dan) of the following rules:

1. REFEREE ABUSE- In accordance with State Youth Soccer Assn. Guidelines, referee abuse is a verbal statement or physical act not resulting in bodily contact that implies or threatens physical harm to a referee or his/ her property. This includes: Yelling at, threatening, bullying, throwing a drink at, coughing the words "bull@#*!" or uttering any phrase that contains the words punch/ beat/ hit/ knock/ slap/ cold-cock/ whack/ smack/ jack-slap/ spank/ put a cap in/ or intimidating an official in any way. Also, this year phrases like: "I'll see you/ get you after the game," constitute threatening language as well. (Are your ears getting red Dan? Hmmmmmm?) Further: Spewing a beverage on an official constitutes a threat.

2. EJECTIONS- Due to the increasing number of ejections statewide, any person being ejected, whether it is a parent, player, or coach, must be "out of sight and sound" of the facility. Any adult that is ejected must COMPLETELY LEAVE THE COMPLEX, players will be placed in a supervised holding-area until the completion of their scheduled game.

Also, Vickie Summers (Madison's mom) found a Malibu Beach Barbie on the field after Wednesday's Advance Skills training. If this belongs to your player, please contact Vickie.

Thanks again, You've all been soooo great! Let's score some goals on Saturday!!!! GO KICKERS!!!!!!!!!

Sincerely, Your Soccer Parent Team Manager/ Snack Coordinator/ Communication Guru (Hannah Jane's Mom) Margo McKlinnish

First Day of School

———•••———

"Are you nervous about going to school for the first time?" I asked Anna, my five-year old, while eating dinner at Carter Bros. BBQ. (This is one of her favorite places –and mine too– so I thought this would be a good spot for our little chat.)

Anna carefully put down her corn dog and looked up, wide-eyed, at me. Slowly, she nodded that curly-topped head of hers up and down in the affirmative. I could tell by the anxious expression on her tiny, five-year-old face, she was nervous about school, really nervous.

I had given a similar pep talk to my two older daughters when they started kindergarten, so I had a rough idea how this would go, but when Anna, my youngest, looked up at me with those big, hazel-colored eyes staring up at me over a half eaten corn dog, it was all I could do not to start crying aloud myself and blubbering uncontrollably.

I wanted to hug her tight and tell her she didn't have to go to that mean old school. I wanted to tell her she would always be my little 'Pepperoni' and I would always be there to protect her, love her and hug her. I wanted to say, "You are my baby girl and I can't believe that you, the littlest of all the Lanes, are actually old enough for real school."

But deep down, I knew this wouldn't do. I knew she was ready for school, even if I wasn't quite ready for her to go.

So I gathered myself together –this took some serious acting on my part– and said, "Well ya know Anna," I tried for an expansive tone of voice, as if I had the whole situation under control. "It's okay to be nervous."

I seemed to have her attention, so I plowed on, "I remember my first day of school. My palms got sweaty. My stomach felt like it had twenty butterflies flapping around in there. My throat was dry. My voice was scratchy. It was awful. But I'm going to tell you something that I didn't realize when it was my first day of school. I didn't know this, but all the other kids in the class are nervous too. Everyone feels nervous."

"Really?" she asked.

"Oh sure," I said in a tone voice I hoped conveyed confidence.

In truth, Anna's first day will be much more of a challenge than mine ever was. This is because, in addition to the new school, the new teacher, and the new children, Anna will also be tackling a new language as well. Like her two older sisters before her, she's enrolled in the Spanish Immersion Program at David D. Jones Elementary School in Greensboro, where, essentially, they speak no English in the classroom.

For this reason, I had a feeling the foreign language thing might be spooking her as well.

"Don't worry too much about the Spanish," I told her. "None of the kids will know Spanish, and they start you off with easy stuff. You'll play games in Spanish. Sing songs in Spanish. Count in Spanish. Your teacher will read you stories in Spanish, and before you know it, you'll be speaking Spanish like you were a real live Guatemalan."

The next morning my wife and I drove Anna to school. Her kindergarten teacher, Señora Castro, greeted Anna –in Spanish- with a big hug and called her by name. (Anna's older sister had Sra. Castro and loved her, so I knew she was in good hands.)

"Do you remember what we talked about last night?" I asked as I hugged her good bye.

Anna nodded and said she did.

Leaving the classroom, I lingered for a moment in the doorway. As I did I caught a glimpse of her curly-topped little head as she cautiously sidled over to the play-mat and began playing with the other children.

There in the hallway, as the tears started sliding down my cheeks, I realized: Anna was going to be fine. It was me who needed some reassurance on the first day of school.

Furious Parkers

———•••———

We Southerners have a reputation for being polite, but all bets are off in the Harris Teeter parking lot on Friday afternoon.

My wife was leaving her grocery store parking space. The lot was crowded with lots of cars in and out. She backed out in front of another car and was admittedly in the wrong. The lady in the other car became furious. She gave my wife the finger, and yelled profanity through the glass. My wife watched horrified, as she could clearly see in the rearview, that she knew the woman. In fact, our children play together, and she was at our house a few days earlier.

It's competitive in the parking lot…..I get it. There are only so many spaces and everyone knows where the best ones are. Gradually the spaces become less desirable the further away from the store you go. We all seek out the closest one and may the best man/woman win. We feel we have suffered a defeat in the battle of life if we don't get that prime spot.

I have an uncle who babies his car. So much so, that he parks it practically in the next county, so people won't be tempted to park next to him and ding his doors. Most of my other relatives think he's nuts or at best eccentric. Actually, I think he has the right idea but for a different reason.

The irony is: Wouldn't we all be better off if we intentionally parked further away and got at least a modicum of exercise in walking to the store. We Americans have a tendency to lap around a parking lot six times –burning gas the whole time– to avoid walking our big fat behinds any precious steps further than necessary.

Also, and I don't want to sound too preachy here…..but let's consider the physical effort we use to get around. We press a button to open the garage door for us. We press a pedal to rush us to speeds 65 miles per hour or faster. We turn a power assisted wheel to steer ourselves in the direction we intend to travel. We complain if the air- conditioning is on too high in our sheltered and climate controlled space. We can travel miles away from our home and back again in comfort without exerting ourselves physically in the least. We can even place a telephone call to someone miles away while driving. Compare this to our ancestors who had to start their journeys by saddling the horse. We have an effortless existence by comparison.

We have it easy –sure– yet it's not good enough. So why do we still cuss out our friends and neighbors in the parking lot.

What has gotten into us? Let's take the woman who cussed at my wife as an example (aside from the fact she is thanking God right now that I am not mentioning her name in this column) maybe she wasn't really mad at my wife. She, no doubt, would be all smiles if my wife accidentally walked in front of her inside the store for example. I'm guessing the problem is that we see each other in parking lots not as other people, our friends and our neighbors, but as competing cars. My wife was just another car that was in her way. She was just yelling at an impersonal vehicle from the security of her own impersonal vehicle.

If the hitching post was full, I doubt people got as mad as we now do in the parking lot. Although I will concede, all the hitching posts that I've seen pictures of were generally right in front of the store.

Mower Mayhem

———•••———

Earlier this summer, I had an unfortunate episode with my fertilizer spreader.

I must have had the toggle set too aggressively, because two days later my grass began dying in a strange pattern. The full extent of the damage was a ten-inch wide stripe of brown death that stretched for about 50 feet in the shape of the letter 'U' in an otherwise lush, green yard.

"Ah no…it's not a crop circle. Mac just has a hard time with the spreader," my wife told a friend.

She knows I have a long history of unfortunate mishaps when it comes to yard equipment.

Over the years I've confessed to mowing over: Tree branches, doggie chew toys, children's shoes, tennis balls, golf balls, a flip flop, a garden hose, a sprinkler nozzle, many rocks, a toy shovel, a large black pipe that is located next to our water meter (I've hit so many times the top gleams a fresh bright brass color each time the mower blade slices into it), and on one particularly lively instance, one of those three pronged metal gardening trowels.

Michele is also familiar with a nasty and well camouflaged tree stump in our backyard that has become my nemesis. Stumps don't normally attack or even move, but I think this one has it in for me. Some days it will crouch low, allowing my mower to glide effortlessly right over top, while at other times the impact of the blade meeting stump-wood can stop the engine cold.

The first time it happened, I went to restart the mower only to find that the impact had bent the shaft so badly the mower wobbled and shook like one of those vibrating belt machines from the 1960's that women used to jiggle their way to a slimmer figure.

The damage was so bad I had to give the mower away, buy a new one, and then I'm embarrassed to say– I hit the same stump a month later, forcing me to buy yet another still. (While I am thankful I didn't become an amputee, Michele refers to that as the "Three Mower Summer.")

On another occasion, I mowed over a nest of yellow jackets. As the insects swarmed all around, I was stung on the ankle and the pain was so unexpected and sharp, I turned loose of the handle, began slapping myself all over, and ran screaming toward the house. The mower eventually ran out of gas.

Despite all this, I really enjoy working in the yard. I like getting out in the fresh air, attempting to make my yard look presentable. In fact, just last night I finished up mowing when Michele said, "It sounded like the mower was making a funny chug-chug sound."

"Well," I said, swallowing hard. "The muffler fell off the mower."

"Ahhh."

"I may be able to put it back on, only I can't tell yet. There was a cloud of black smoke when it fell off, and the muffler itself was so hot it was smoking. I couldn't pick it up."

"So what did you do with it?" she asked.

"Left it there."

"Smoking in the grass? Won't the lawn catch fire?"

I tried to sound confident as I said, "Do I look like someone who would set fire to the lawn?" But as I spoke, I was actually thinking, fire may be the only disaster that hasn't befallen the Lane lawn yet...but there are still a few weeks of summer left.

Fla-Vor-Ice Pops

—●●●—

"Hey Dad, can I have a popsicle?" my six year old daughter, Anna, asked.

"Do we have any popsicles?" I said, knowing that my wife rarely, if ever, buys sugary sweets for the kids.

"Uhh huuh," she said vigorously nodding her small head up and down. "Mom bought lots of them. There's some in the freezer, and a whole lot more in the basement." She was now hopping up and down with anticipation as I handed her one of the frozen treats.

As I said, normally, my wife is a sensible shopper, but apparently, in some temporary lapse of sanity, she brought home a giant box of Fla-Vor-Ice Pops as a summer treat for our three girls.

This was a bad-buy on so many different levels; I scarcely know where to begin.

First, the sheer quantity of my wife's blunder is dumbfounding.

As Anna, my wee informant, alluded to –the box was indeed in the basement. I had no trouble finding it as it was bright and fruity colored and so large a house cat might fit comfortably inside. It contained 200 individual 1.5 ounce pops and the label boasted a total weight of 19 pounds. If you do the math, this works out to 6.3 pounds of colored sugar-water per child. Forgive me, but I think even in a hot month like June, 6.3 pounds of popsicles per child may be a tad excessive.

Secondly, with 66 popsicles each on hand, the kids can't contain themselves. They think they've hit the Sugar-Lottery as this is such a rare and unprecedented treat. They've been gorging themselves on seven, eight and sometimes nine pops per day in such delightful flavors as: **Lively-Lime**, **Tongue-Dye-Blue**, **Spillable-Strawberry**, **Scrub-Resistant-Grape**, **No-Way-This-Stain-Is-Coming-Out-of-the-Carpet-Orange**, and **That-Shirt-Is-Definitely-Ruined-Tropical Punch**.

And, as if that's not bad enough, opening a Fla-Vor-Ice pop requires cutting the plastic sleeve on one end. Scissors work the best for this job, but with three kids all clamoring for their seventh and eighth popsicle of the day, these excited, sugar-buzzed, children often have difficulty waiting their turn. They've taken to wielding long, dangerously sharp kitchen knives to slice open the pops often splashing the frozen contents on floor and clothing in the process. So far we've had no blood spilled, but I do imagine entire battalions of ants are on the march into our kitchen as we speak.

Thirdly, the ingredients include such goodies as: High Fructose Corn Syrup, Artificial Flavors, Sodium Benzoate, Potassium Sorbate, Red #40, Yellow #5 and #6, Blue #1, and some sort of fish paralyzer. (I made that last one up, but you get the idea.)

Knowing this Popsicle Banquet must soon come to an end, I decided to make my stand.

One quick tour through the house and yard produced about a dozen discarded sleeves. I immediately called a meeting of the children. Brandishing the sticky plastic wrappers in the air, I gave them an ultimatum. "If I find one more of these...anywhere...other than in the trash can...I'm taking away the popsicles for good."

Later that evening, I found two: A discarded lime wrapper and a strawberry that had been left on top of the cocktail table in the den. This is it, problem solved, I thought with a wicked smile.

I just hope that when winter comes, my normally sensible wife doesn't buy a dump-truck load of hot cocoa.

Make Up Your Mind Tar Heel Fans

———•••———

Dad and I went to many, many UNC games throughout my childhood, and over the years I learned, that even though cursing wasn't allowed, I could shout "Go to Hell State" and my father would never reprimand me. In fact, quite the opposite, he seemed pleased. It was as if he and I knew that NC State was so loathsome, so vile and so reprehensible, that this superseded the normal household rules about bad language.

We both understood this. In fact, everyone wearing light blue understands this….. or at least I thought they did?

What brings this to mind is that Dad and I, along with a family friend, Barry Frank, went to a UNC football game yesterday.

So, it was us and seven other Tar Heels there.

OK I'm kidding. There were twelve of us.

Just being back in Kenan Stadium on that bright sunny day reminded me of the first game Dad and I went to back when I was about seven or eight. In those days, when the marching band broke into the fight song "I'm a Tar Heel Born" everyone, and I mean everyone, in the stadium shouted "GO TO HELL STATE" at the top of their lungs. It was unanimous, and there was no debate that NC State should be the school that everyone hated the most.

But yesterday, the UNC fans in our section couldn't seem to make up their minds exactly whom they wanted to go to Hell. Half the crowd shouted "Go to Hell State" while the other half shouted "Go to Hell Duke."

What's up with that?

First, in my mind, eternal damnation is a pretty big thing, and if you are going to suggest someone to go there, the least you can do is get a consensus.

Secondly, the statement isn't very specific. I mean what if this Go-to-Hell request was actually granted? Would it just apply to just the football team? Would the coaches be included? Would the cheerleaders also be required to face an eternity of hell-fire and damnation as well? The whole student body? Would the professors go to Hell too? I guess it could apply to everyone….. including alumni?

This is where I want to call a timeout. My neighbor, John Kennett, went to NC State, and even has a Wolfpack sticker on his car. He's a really nice guy. His daughter, Katie, and my daughter play together, and if it's all the same to you, as a Go-to-Hell-Shouting-Tar-Heel-fan, I'd like to put John in for an exemption if this Go-to-Hell thing ever comes about.

Also, my pastor went to Duke. I can't imagine him going to Hell based on the whim of a bunch of Carolina fans.

So, now that I'm a father of three, and old enough to cuss on my own without being worried about getting reprimanded by my father…..I can't help thinking how silly the whole "Go-to-Hell" thing sounds anyhow.

When you really think about it, it's really quite silly.

And I'd like to be able to recommend something else, but must admit, I don't have a better alternative.

I understand that it's important to Tar Heel fans to convey the extreme amount of loathing you feel towards these rival schools. I get that. But I have to say, nothing is working.

I can't imagine shouting: "WE REALLY, REALLY DISLIKE YOU DUKE."

Pretty lame.

Or "WE WISH YOU PEOPLE AT NC STATE WOULD ALL JUST DIE OR GO SOMEWHERE FAR AWAY." Clumsy, weak and too wordy.

Even if I could think of a better alternative, to the "Go to Hell Duke…or State" I have doubts UNC fans would embrace it anyway.

I mean, if you can't agree on who you want to go to Hell the most, then what can you agree on?

Fish, Fish and More Fish

———•••———

Cannon, my twelve year-old daughter, and I left town early Friday morning: Playing hooky, we were bound for The Georgia Aquarium in Atlanta.

As I drove down I-85, I recalled the first aquarium I ever owned. I was 11 years old, had saved my money and bought a used 10 gallon set-up from Chip Cecil, a friend and classmate, for twenty dollars.

This was the beginning of my becoming a bona fide fish nerd.

Scouring and practically memorizing Simon and Schuster's "Guide to Tropical Fish", I made my selections carefully. I studied the size and temperament and compatibility of each fish. One corydora catfish, three zebra danios, a silver and black angelfish and a lone male guppy (of the feeder-fish variety that somehow wound up in the bag with the catfish accidentally) were my first inhabitants.

As I grew, so did the size of my aquariums. By high school, I was up to a 20 gallon tall. After college, I bought my first 55. By the time my wife and I were engaged, I was sporting a 55, a 65 and a 90 gallon. Plus, I had graduated from fresh water to salt. Reef tanks with live corals, I've done it all.

One would think, when this giant aquarium opened in Atlanta about two years ago, I would have been among the first through the door. But actually, I've been to many of the big aquariums, and have been let down too many times. For example: Ripley's at Myrtle Beach was a huge disappointment. Many of the fish, I found, had head and lateral line disease, which is caused by high nitrates in the water. Nitrates build up over time from lack of proper water changes and, simply put, when this condition is present, it means the fish are swimming around in a high concentration of their own waste.

So it was that Cannon and her smug, fish-nerd father entered The Georgia Aquarium.

Once inside, and after we'd toured all five of the exhibit areas, I called my wife hardly able to contain my excitement, "This place is unbelievable!" I said. "They've got six million gallons of water in here, and it's extremely well done. We've seen sea turtles, piranha, penguins, Beluga whales, sting rays, saw fish, six foot grouper and the reef tanks are amazing. They've also got this Deep Ocean exhibit with four whale sharks in it…and it's soo big you can't even see them all at once. Imagine four whale sharks, each about 20 feet long and you can't even see them until they swim by. You have to sit and wait for them. It's unbelievable. Cannon's into it as well…she loves it. She's taken about 200 pictures with our camera. It's like we've both died and gone to the Great Barrier Reef."

"I'm surprised you like it," she said. "You usually hate those big aquariums. You walk around poo-pooing everything…pointing out how sick the fish are."

"Yeah. Well I haven't seen any disease here."

Actually, this wasn't quite true. I had noticed one disease going around in Atlanta. It was a strong case of Fish Fever and it was contracted by a twelve-year-old and her smug, fish-nerd dad.

True Love Has It's Evening

——•••——

These are ordinary men: dentists, teachers, contractors, bankers, and business-men, who have one thing in common......their love for their daughters.

And tonight they stand together, lights dimmed low, in a ballroom. The corsage he bought compliments the white silk gown she is wearing.

Red and white balloons are scattered throughout the dancehall; the starched tablecloths are sprinkled with Valentine confetti, in keeping with the sweet-heart theme.

The mirror-ball showers them with a rainfall of light as other smartly dressed couples around them are rocking tenderly to the slow rhythms. He thinks to him-self, how did God create such beauty?

And she is beautiful.

Each man at this magical dance loves his girl completely. He loves her with a type of love that he never considered possible.

When she is sad, he listens. When she triumphs, he shares in her joy. She knows he will always love and adore her and treat her with respect.

She smiles up at him with the certain knowledge of their love.

The song is The Temptation's "My Girl" and it's so perfect he wants to cry.

Most of these dads deal with the difference in height by completely picking up their diminutive dance partners, allowing their small legs to dangle back and forth in the air as they sway to the tunes.

The style of dancing may vary from couple to couple, but the feelings are the same on this special night.

The Sweetheart Ball is the highlight of the year and it's a credit to the guys in our town, because - wanting this night to be extra special- they have made all the arrangements.

It's a night where the fathers of our town hold a ball just for their daughters.

The High Point North Carolina YMCA Sweetheart Ball is held every year on the Saturday before Valentine's Day and-I speak with experience- is a magical night where the fathers get dressed up in their best suits and the girls are attired in equal fashion. There's a meal, a photographer and corsages. It's just like a real prom only better because there are no tears, broken hearts or booze like there was at mine.

It tickles me to lookout across the dance floor seeing these guys, who seem as large as giants dancing with these miniature young ladies.

I guess what really makes the Sweetheart Ball so special for me is that as a father you know the day will come, the day when your little girl will be all grown and dancing with another.

As a dad, all you can do is enjoy this moment. And hope that her future dancing partner will be as wonderful as she deserves.

A Dotted Calendar?

——•••——

I long for a relaxing weekend.

I positively ache to just kick-back and unwind. Watch a football game perhaps.

But it's not to be.

Saturday and Sunday: I don't even have time to turn on the television.

On most weekends, here lately, it seems I'm on the go more than a presidential candidate with bladder control problems.

In an effort to tame our often unruly schedule, my wife has taken to placing different colored stickers on the family calendar. Orange sticker-dots are for me, yellow dots for our middle daughter, and green for my youngest ....or maybe green is my color....I can't honestly remember, but what I can tell you is that our weekends look like they have the multi-colored, sticker-dot measles.

Orange dot- Halloween party at the Williams's. Green dot: Sell pumpkins at the church. Yellow dot: Sleep-over birthday party. School trip on the 17th...Indian Princesses Campout on the 18th....on and on and on.

I'm not whining...okay maybe I am whining a little bit. We are all healthy and lead full active lives, I just wish that one weekend, every now and then wasn't so full and active.

The most disappointing realization is that I thought I'd get a break once my oldest daughter went to college.

She played youth soccer, so our weekends were booked often years in advance with club season, school season, in-door season, tournaments and practices. When you're a soccer parent, you expect for your weekends to be "soccerized" —meaning we couldn't go anywhere without checking the soccer calendar first.

But now, since there's no more soccer, where is all this free time I'm supposed to have?

My wife and I both know that we've only got ourselves to blame.

Every dot on the calendar was put up there by either her or me. And it was put up there for a reason.

It means that whatever IT is, it means that at least one of us thinks it's worthwhile.

If it wasn't worthwhile, then we wouldn't have signed-up or committed ourselves to go in the first place.

In short, we put it up there because we wanted to go or because we thought that there would be some benefit to going.

As for a solution, I think what we need, and this is going to sound a bit ridiculous, is to schedule in some time to relax during the weekend.

We need to deliberately set aside some stay-at-home-and-do-nothing time. Time to just kick-back and relax.

We could even find a new color: a relaxing taupe color sticker-dot perhaps.

And looking across the calendar, I think we've got a 15-minute opening November 19th.

Maybe I can kick-back and relax then?

Back to School

—•••—

Ah, back to school time.

For weeks my daughters have been pestering me to take them shopping for school supplies and for weeks I've been dreading it.

For me, buying school supplies is nearly as bad as Christmas shopping. It's the same long lines, the same crowded stores; the only difference is, with back-to-school shopping, the kids get to come along. And as I've come to learn, my daughters have a tendency to deliberate with the intensity of someone facing painful surgery as to whether they should select the notebook with the adorable basket of kittens on the cover or the one with the tropical sunset design. This typically turns the whole experience into a rather lengthy affair.

With a sense of apprehension, I started the car. The girls, on the other hand, clapped their hands in small rapid-fire bursts; visibly bouncing up and down in the back seat with excitement as we drove along.

Within the store, we were directed to a special 'Back to School' department positively brimming with every conceivable item for youthful scholarship. The girls squealed with delight as they produced their lists and went to work.

They hustled about, darting up and down the aisles, with the energy of a contestant in one of those supermarket style game shows where the object is to rake as much loot as possible into the shopping basket before the time runs out.

I feared that this trip might get really, really expensive, so I appointed myself as a sort of make shift guardian-of-the-shopping-cart, afraid that if I glanced away for even one moment some frivolous item might appear.

All in all, the girls were actually doing quite well, only selecting the prescribed items. But as the pile of stuff grew larger and larger, my forehead started to perspire as I was starting to get a sense of the sheer dollar volume that was involved here.

On about her eighth or ninth trip back to the cart, my daughter dropped a pair of scissors in the buggy. Seeing an opportunity for some savings, I asked, "Where are your scissors from last year?"

"Daaaad. My scissors from last year are blue."

"And what's so terrible about blue scissors?"

"Uhh, Daaaad. The theme this year is green!" This was spoken in a tone of voice which seemed to imply that I am totally out of touch with all reality on this planet.

I considered telling her how it was in my day. I considered telling her how my elementary teacher would bring out a box of metal scissors from a high shelf in some dusty cupboard and how all the kids would clamor around the up-ended box, scrambling to grab a pair that had the least amount of rust and dried crud on it. (I also recall the scissors themselves; being so dull, they didn't so much cut the construction paper as, fold it into ninety degree angles as you went.)

But alas, I didn't want to sound like one of those dreaded stereotypical dads who reputedly tell their kids about how tough they had it –walking five miles to school in the snow and all that– so I bit my tongue.

I just pray that when she gets ready to shopping for college the same thing won't occur. I can imagine myself asking: "So where's your laptop from freshman year, you know, the one I paid $3,500.00 for?"

"Uhhh, Daaaad. I need…like…a new one. The theme for this year is green."

The Words We Choose...

———•••———

I was recounting a tale to my three daughters around the dinner table when my wife suddenly interrupted me.

"Don't say that word in front of the children," she said.

"Don't say what," I asked.

"That word," she said more forcefully.

With the possible exception of the time I nearly impaled myself with a power drill while falling off a step ladder, I can't recall ever using any real profanity in front of the children. We simply avoid bad language in the Lane house.

But apparently, I had said a bad word –at least in my wife's opinion.

I had been telling my kids about a scene in a movie where a woman kicks a man "in the between the legs," and had used the word *crotch* in the telling.

Even though I tend to be a little more relaxed about these things than my wife, until this very moment, I had never considered this particular word inappropriate in any way. (Let the record show that according to the *American Heritage Dictionary* the word *crotch* is defined as: "The angle or region of the angle formed by the junction of two parts or members, such as two branches or legs.")

While in a strict sense, *crotch* is not a curse word, I know what my wife meant. She was imagining our seven-year old going to school and yelling, "crotch, crotch, crotch" down the hallway. And I agree, in that context, the word does have an improper ring to it.

But this conversation did bring up an interesting point: what about those words that are in the gray area, the ones that are not exactly polite, but yet are not quite profanity either?

We've had instances of this sort in our house over the years. My middle daughter, when she was about 6-years old, started yelling out the names of various animals, like rabbit and mouse, then and this is the funny part– her choices evolved into phrases like "CHICKEN HOLE" and a few seconds later, she yelled, "PIG SQUIRT." Also, I should mention we were at a public swimming pool. My first reaction was of horror. But as I thought about it more carefully, I considered, she may have thought chickens lived in holes. Plus, there was no maliciousness in her voice. She was just goofing around. And why would a rabbit hole, or a gopher hole be any different than a chicken hole? Just as long as no animals that bray are involved, I thought it would be okay. As for 'pig squirt', I had no idea where that came from, but I confess, I kind'a liked the novelty of it.

In the end, I decided to let it go, even though both 'chicken hole' and 'pig squirt' would have, at least in my wife's eyes, failed the school hallway test.

As for my crotch faux pas, the children sensed an opening: "What's wrong with CROTCH?" "Yeah mom, why can't we say the word CROTCH? There's nothing wrong with CROTCH," they pressed.

Fuming, my wife glared at me from across the table.

In an effort to make peace in the house, I went to the kids later in the evening and implored them not to say the word, ever again, only my middle daughter, devilishly, held her cell phone behind her back as I gave my little homily.

I wasn't aware her cell phone even had a record feature until I heard my own my voice filling the house: "Don't say the word *crotch*, it's not polite," over and over again as all three children reeled with laughter.

"I'm not saying it," she added with a gleeful expression. "DAD IS!" as she pressed play again and again.

Of course, my wife was furious while I was actually relieved. I was relieved I didn't say anything worse.

Super Saucy Man

———•••———

When I was little, I dressed as Batman for something like five straight Halloweens. As I grew older, I collected *Spiderman* and *Fantastic Four* comic books. (Note to self —ask mom where they are.)

I've always had a soft spot for super-heroes, so when the new Disney movie *The Incredibles* came out, featuring a family of super heroes who -for fear of lawsuits- are forced to go into hiding and disguise their super abilities. I bought the DVD on the first day. I bought it under the auspices of it being a gift for my daughters. In truth, I think they enjoyed it, but I suspect not as much as me.

In addition to being a fabulous movie, it got me to thinking about my own family. I started wondering: maybe the Lanes have some disguised super powers?

For example, I have a super-human appetite for sauces of all kinds. For me, those dainty thimble-sized paper condiment cups most fast food restaurants offer are entirely inadequate for my needs. I require at least a cereal bowl's worth of ketchup with each order of fries.

With my passion for sauces, I could easily imagine myself changing from a mild-mannered salesman by day into a super alter-ego around meal time. I haven't settled on my super-hero name yet, but a few possibilities that come to mind are: Super Teriyaki Man or The Masked Mayonnaise Marvel, or The Great Gravy Guru, The Lone Remoulade Ranger, Rib Rub Rambo, The Caped Catsup Crusader, The Amazing Au Jus or perhaps The Horseradish Honcho.

Whichever name I choose, my super hero outfit could include a yellow necktie that I ruined in an unfortunate soy sauce spill a few years back. Plus, I have a collection of shirts and pants soiled with similarly ruinous stains and the super-saucy outfit might allow me to get some additional wear out of them. Honestly, I don't know if I could do any good deeds or fight any crime as a masked marvel, but I'm certain I could capture the flavor of a good steak with some Heinz 57 or make an order of chicken wings more arresting with a smattering of Texas Pete, but that would probably be about as far as it goes.

For my wife, Michele, one possibility could be: (And I'll have to be careful not to let her read this before it goes to print.) Veto Woman for her God-given talent to say "no." For example, when we were newly-weds, I badly wanted to hang a mounted Marlin over the mantle I had caught in Florida. All was well until the mighty Veto Woman exercised her special super powers. My stuffed fish now hangs over the mantle; only it's 200 miles away in my father's beach house at Wrightsville.

Another possibility for Michele could be The Sonic Sneezer. I've noticed some women are embarrassed to sneeze out loud and hold their noses in an attempt internally to contain the force of the sneeze. I worry that these people's eyeballs are going to pop out. Suppressing that much energy inside one's own cranium has got to be painful. Michele, however, lets it all out. Even as petite as she is, she can nearly break the sound barrier with the force of her nasal eruptions.

I think the two of us, as super-heroes, could make quite a pair. I imagine my wife and I together in search of adventure as we add various sauces to foods and sneeze voluminously about town in our super-hero outfits. Maybe we could star in our own comic book series. It could be like a dream of my youth actually coming true.

The only problem I can foresee is that we'd have to leave Veto Woman out. She's not very agreeable, plus, she would probably think the whole idea of pretending to be super-heroes is silly. Really silly.

This Thing in the Backyard

———•••———

The problem started a few weeks back when my two youngest began construction of a homemade fort in the back yard.

What began as a small, ramshackle lean-to has grown rapidly into a sprawling pavilion with each passing weekend as more and more kids from the neighborhood have joined in the fun.

On any given Saturday, a whole warren of children can be seen scurrying in and out of this kid-crafted wigwam and dragging an alarming amount of building materials into my yard. Scrap cloth for roofing, picnic benches for support, broom handles as joists, sticks, logs, old bricks, and an aluminum step ladder have all been used in the construction….so far.

Last weekend, I spotted Trey, the boy from next door, hauling in a load of lumber and I thought I heard the sound of a skill-saw off in the distance.

The problem is: I don't know where to draw the line.

On the one hand, I think it's wonderful. The children have built this thing all by themselves with zero help from the grown-ups. I think there is something to be said for that sort of ingenuity. From my own experience making tree houses as a youngster, I know this home-made fort can be transformed: into a castle rivaling King Arthur's; an outpost in the Wild West; or a ship crashing through the waves. It can be whatever their lively young minds dream it to be.

On the other, (and this is my unimaginative, 40 year old homeowner brain at work) I can't help but see what a colossal mess my backyard has become.

From a distance, it looks like a slap-dash heap of sagging, mismatched fabric, in colors that would make Martha Stewart cringe. Up close it looks worse. Olive green, bright purple and leopard print fabrics have perhaps never before been seen in such close proximity.

The children are also using an old wash tub to store all their discarded roofing fabric, only, after the recent rains we've had, the tub now looks more like a giant rusting bowl of textile soup. Plus, an area of grass big enough to park a Suburban is, I fear, permanently kaput.

So unless you are, say, younger than 12-years old, the whole thing is becoming really quite painful to look at.

And to make matters worse, my next door neighbor had a class reunion party on his back deck last weekend. The deck has an unfortunate view of my yard and I could imagine his guests glancing toward my house and asking, "What is that? Is your neighbor building a refugee camp?" or worse, "If the yard looks that bad on the outside, I wonder what the inside looks like?"

I desperately want to tear this mismatched shanty down, bag it up, and haul it to the dump, but, I confess, I don't have the heart.

I know this home-made fort might not look like a castle to me, but I'm pretty sure it represents something quite special to the kids.

I think maybe, I'll leave it up for a time, but, for safety reasons, I really would like to know if that was a skill-saw I heard the other day.

Snoring Helplessly

———•••———

GRANDFATHER MOUNTIAN, NC -At approximately 4:00 AM Sunday morning, High Point resident, Mac Lane, was evicted from the small camping tent he shared with his wife Michele after failing to contain his vigorous snoring.

Lane's wife had reportedly made several attempts in the night to encourage Mr. Lane to cease his snoring activity including: poking Mr. Lane in the ribs; elbowing Mr. Lane in the small of the back; using her hip and buttocks to 'bump' Mr. Lane as he lay sleeping; and finally, grabbing Mr. Lane by the shoulder and shaking him forcefully while whispering through gritted teeth "Pleeeeeease… Mac. You've got to roll over on your side. You are snoring right into my ear….I haven't slept all night."

All of Mrs. Lane's efforts proved unsuccessful however.

"He just wouldn't stop," Mrs. Lane said. "On and on and on. He was making this sound right in my ear, and it was sooo loud. I hated to do it, but I told him it was either him or me. One of us was going to have to sleep in the car."

At approximately 4:00 AM, a confused and beleaguered Mr. Lane emerged, barefoot and shirtless, from the couple's tent onto the dark and rain-soaked campsite clutching a pillow, an unrolled sleeping bag and a small reading light.

The nearly naked Lane wandered aimlessly for some time while aiming the tiny light into the inky darkness, until, he was eventually able to locate the dark silhouette of what he believed to be his black Honda Pilot.

Lane approached the car delicately holding both the pillow and the sleeping bag high into the air to minimize contact with the soggy weeds and brush.

It wasn't until the car's automatic door locks failed to respond to repeated clicks from the keyless entry pad, did Lane realize that he was attempting to unlock his friend Michael Amos's car and not his own. Lane's black Honda was parked some distance behind and to the right of Amos's.

"I know Michael drives a car similar to mine," Lane admitted. "We'd been camping with his family, the Thompsons and the Yorks all weekend. I guess I just wasn't thinking clearly at that hour."

Lane's feet and legs were reportedly sopping wet and miserably cold by the time he eventually unlocked his own automobile.

"In a way I was relieved," he said recounting the ordeal. "My wife had been hitting me all night in the tent and yelling at me to roll over. The car was uncomfortable mostly because that seat belt thing jabbed me in the back, but it was better than having my wife elbow me in the ribs all night."

According to the owner's manual, Lane's 2007 Honda Pilot is not designed for sleeping and offers no amenities for prone occupants.

Mr. Lane has a history of snoring helplessly and has been cited by his wife and three daughters on numerous occasions in the past. His previous infractions have occurred most recently after Lane returned home from a trade-show in Las Vegas, during a recent trip to Myrtle Beach and on a Thursday night where nothing particularly exciting was going on.

School Trip Is Not So Bad

———•••———

Have you ever had one of those moments in life where you ask yourself, "What the heck am I doing?"

Well, I'm having one of those moments right now. It's 4:30 in the morning and my middle daughter and I left the house before sunrise; before the newspaper; and before anyone who isn't a vampire should be awake.

As I backed the car out into the inky darkness, I said to her, "Well there is one good thing about leaving this early. There won't be any traffic."

At 5:15 AM we arrived at my daughter's school in Greensboro where we were assigned to charter bus number three. After stowing our suitcases, we boarded a bus which was already filled with noisy and excited fifth graders.

I made my way to the back and I spotted another parent chaperone. "Hi. I'm Chris," he said. "If you're going to sit back here, you can help me guard the bathroom. Make sure no one uses it. I've been on five of these trips, and you have no idea how bad this bus can smell after three days if we let the kids go potty back here."

I liked this guy instantly. But upon hearing him, say the word 'potty,' I suddenly had to go potty myself and the bus hadn't even left. I worried I might not make it to the first stop. Panicking slightly, I glanced around. At this hour, the school building is locked and from the look on this guy Chris' face, I think I'd have to fight him to get to the toilet once we were in route. In desperation, I exited the bus, walked some distance across the parking lot, and went behind the school's library –but please don't tell anyone as I'm pretty sure this is in violation of a whole host of rules.

I made it back to the bus just as our driver was introducing himself, and I must say, the name "Wild Bill" is not the sort of name that instills a great deal of confidence when navigating a twenty ton, sixty-foot long bus, filled with scores of children along the steep and winding roads of the North Carolina Mountains.

Wild Bill was at the wheel, the Toilet Watchdog Dad at the rear, and forty-seven fifth graders (each armed with a Nintendo D.S. Game Boy), seven parent chaperones; one teacher; and me sandwiched somewhere in between. We explored Bryson City, Cherokee, Nantahala, and Asheville. We rode the Great Smoky Mountain Railway, toured the Biltmore House and winery, mined for gems and explored Linville Caverns over the next three days.

Like any trip, there were moments of pure agony, like when Watch Dog Dad and I were starving and found ourselves dead last in line (139th and 140th) at the J&S Cafeteria in Asheville. But there were some good moments as well, like when I discovered that even among her school friends, my daughter is not too old, or too embarrassed, to hold my hand.

All in all, it was a much better trip than expected. The teachers were wonderful, the kids –without exception– behaved themselves, and the adults, aside from the occasional injury and stopped-up toilet in the hotel room, fared pretty well too.

So, if this becomes an annual event, and the kids go on another three-day school trip next year, I'd like to make a few suggestions:

1. A port-a-potty in the parking lot for those sudden departure needs.

2. Can someone let Wild Bill's bus eat first at the restaurants? Just once?

Teenage-Girls-All-Talking-At-Once Party

———•••———

Can someone tell me why it's called a Slumber Party?

My wife doesn't slumber. I don't slumber. The dog doesn't slumber, and most importantly, the numerous teenage girls who are lying in sleeping bags on nearly every flat surface of our den certainly don't slumber, or at least not for very long.

A more accurate name for this kind of party would be: an Endurance Party or a Great-Number-of-Fourteen-Year-Old-Girls-All-Talking-And-Texting-At-Once Party.

I'm sorry. I don't mean to sound too sour, but I've been awake for a really long time and I'm feeling about as cheerful as the soggy birthday cake I just scraped into the trash can.

I knew my wife and I were in trouble when, about two weeks ago, we saw the list.

I counted fifteen names.

"Um," I said to my daughter. "Do you think your guest list might be a tad long? Where are we going to put that many girls?"

My daughter had a very rational reason for inviting each girl on the list, plus I could tell she had put a lot of time into this. This added to the fact that my wife and I completely caved and didn't make her shorten the list, meant that we had just condoned inviting an extraordinary amount of girls into our home. (Although, I must secretly confess we desperately hoped that at least one, two or perhaps as many as eight of these girls would have other plans.)

On the morning of the party, I asked my daughter who all was coming.

"It's complicated," she said or something to that effect.

Later, I learned what she meant by complicated.

It turns out that many of the girls did have other plans, but strangely, they also came to my daughter's party as well. What this meant was that we had a steady stream of girls who were either arriving or departing almost constantly during the entire course of the event.

Just when I thought I had everyone's name memorized, someone would depart or arrive or one would leave and totally throw me off.

The party itself seemed to go well. The girls listened to music, texted each other, and played games.

At Spooky Woods of Terror, we lost two and picked up one. (It's complicated.)

From there we drove back to the house where the girls texted each other; ate cake and ice cream; and texted each other some more.

At one point I asked my daughter, "Who are you texting?"

"Sara," she said.

"But isn't Sara standing right there?"

"Yes. She is," as she burst into a fit of giggling. "Isn't this great!"

And so it went. Talking and texting. Texting and talking.

There was so much texting going on, a passer-by might have thought our house had been taken over by an army of electronic communication specialists.

At mid-night I went upstairs, and at 1:00 AM, I could still hear them downstairs "chatting away."

I must have closed my eyes for a time, because when I awoke around 3:30, the TV was still audible, but there were no girls' voices.

Bleary-eyed, I made my way downstairs and clicked off the TV set, and it was only then that I noticed a strange thing in my house ....silence.

Ahh...I thought....now this is a Slumber Party.

Soccer Heat

———•••———

My daughter just joined a new soccer team. This was my first chance to meet the new parents. I wanted to make a good impression since I would be spending an inordinate amount of time with these people over the next several months, but I fear I got off to a shaky start.

The trouble started with my wife and my cooler, of all things.

Before I left the house and knowing it was going to be a scorcher, I packed the cooler with bottled waters, cans of Sprite and loads of ice.

The weather didn't disappoint; it was sweltering.

The first game at ten o'clock proved to be a warm-up for the two o'clock match-up. This game was to be played on a field surrounded by trees where we parents felt nary a puff of breeze. The 97 degrees felt downright brutal.

My wife, Michele, who truly loathes hot weather, joined me and the two of us sat in our folding chairs with all the other roasting parents.

Mid-way through the first half, Michele suddenly kicked off her flip-flops, and opened my cooler, and dipped her feet inside for some relief. She made an 'ahhhh' sound as she smiled and wiggled her toes about in the icy water.

Inspired by my wife's foot bath, I removed my baseball cap and plunged it into the icy cooler's water. I held the hat under water for a while, my hands bumping the floating bottles and cans as I sloshed it around. I wrung the hat out a few times like a wash cloth, dipped it in again, and placed the sopping cap back on my head, savoring the blissfully chilly water as it dripped down my face and neck.

Throughout the rest of the first half, my wife's feet danced in and out of the cooler and my cap made the plunge five or six more times.

At some point, I reached into the cooler and grabbed a water bottle for myself. As I was about to take a drink, I noticed another soccer mom eyeing me. Instinctively, and without thinking, I offered her one, but it wasn't until she began twisting off the cap did I realize -with horror- I had wrung my nasty salt and sweat crusted cap in and out of the very liquid her beverage had been floating in just a few minutes prior. Plus, the cooler had also been a swimming pool for my wife's feet.

I had a split second to decide if I should tell her or not. I'd only just met this woman and knew I'd be seeing her nearly every weekend for the next six months. I was terrified she might think we were some sort of barefoot bumpkins who regularly bathe in our Igloo. I still had a chance to make a good first impression, if I kept my mouth shut.

In the end, I decided to come clean. I thought she needed to know. "Uhhh…You may not want that water after all," I said gesturing toward the cooler and feeling rather like an idiot, "my wife's feet have been inside there and I wrung my hat in and out of it several times…. in the cooler water that is."

She shrugged and took a sip from the bottle anyway.

I guess it was just that hot of a day.

Those Little Secrets

———•••———

Sorry, but I may have to cut this short because both my wife and I are seriously stressed ever since we agreed to rent our house for Furniture Market.

If you haven't ever become homeless and voluntarily allowed your house to be invaded by out of town furniture people, you may be thinking to yourself: so what's the big deal? Yeah, you clean up; put some fresh towels out. No sweat. I could handle that?

But what you may not know is that it's not the cleaning. It's not the packing up. It's not the fact that we'll be voluntarily homeless for 10 days that got us in such a knot. And it's not the fact that, in our case, a bunch of bedding and pillow executives will be sleeping in our beds, and microwaving in our microwave that's gotten us so stressed.

No, the real reason goes much deeper and is significantly more sinister. The real reason we stress is that our house has all sorts of little hidden secrets that we are afraid – no terrified– the renters will discover.

You see, we haven't rented in 5 years and in that time we've been cultivating strange blotches of red and black colored mildew on the ceiling in the girls' bathroom. So, do we re-paint? Re-sheet rock? No time.

Also, the Lanes do not own a complete set of drinking glasses. Now, if each glass were a different size and shape, maybe just maybe, we could pass them off as us being eclectic or somehow artsy. But what we've got is half a set of modern tall ones and a half a set of traditional and stylistically incompatible shorts ones, which means that somewhere along the line we've combined two separate sets because over the years. We've broken some of one and some of the other. This is definitely not artsy and definitely not eclectic, rather this is my wife and I being too cheap to spring for new ones. The same goes for salad bowls- three. Soup bowls -seventeen. I'm not sure how that happened, but our glasses and dishware are a total mess.

Plus, our dishwasher is kaput. Combine this with the fact the ice maker in the fridge is broken since....well....I can't remember.

And, last summer, I scratched a series of mosquito bites on my leg until they bled and subsequently, the sheets in the master bedroom have little scrub-resistant red dots of dried blood all over them. "It's gross and we can't let the renters sleep on these," my wife said. And she's right. So, add a new set of sheets to the list.

And there is the unavoidable fact that each time one opens the front door, our orange tabby cat Tiger, attempts to leap inside.

There is also the chair in the dining room that still shows the stain of where that devil of a child, six-year old Hannah McKlinnish, dumped her chocolate cupcake in her lap and didn't tell anyone until we discovered that she'd been sitting in it -or on it- for the duration of the party and subsequently smeared cake and icing into the upholstery fabric of the chair. And to this day, one can still see -quite clearly- a chocolate cupcake colored stain.

So instead of sitting here writing this, I really need to get back to work. I've got a cat to kill.....kidding.... well, maybe not kidding.....of course I'm kidding.... and mildew to scrub, and drinking glasses to worry over and all these other little things that are so terribly wrong with our house.

Oh, and please do me a favor. If you know any bedding executives from the DC area, I hope you can keep these things a secret. Particularly about the mildew..... and the blood on the sheets thing.

That's really gross and I'd hate for them to find out.

Trouble at the Self-Checkout

———•••———

There are many, many things I'm not very good at: backing up trailers, dancing, and growing hair on the top of my head –to name just a few. But perhaps the one thing that gives me the most trouble here lately is using these self-checkout lanes that you see everywhere nowadays.

I make a complete mess of it nearly every time.

Take yesterday as an example. My wife was in the middle of cooking dinner and came up short on a few ingredients. My plan was to dash to the grocery in a gallant fashion. As I put my keys in the ignition, I was picturing in my mind how grateful and appreciative she would be. I imagined on my return, she might give me a big kiss for my heroics.

With no time for a buggy, I grabbed a basket and like some crazy middle-aged man in a high-speed Easter Egg hunt, I dashed here and there. I raced to the checkout and saw all the lanes had long, long lines. So, swallowing hard, I approached the self-checkout area.

This never goes well for me. I'm sure hundreds maybe thousands of people use this method of check-out every day without incident, but alas, I am not one of them. Somehow, I always manage to get the machine that only takes cash, or doesn't take cash, or doesn't accept any sort of payment at all.

Surprisingly, when my turn came, I got off to a pretty good start. I scanned the first two items with no mishaps, but the trouble started when I waved my bundle of cilantro in front of the electric eye thingamajiggy. Nothing happened. I waved harder. Still nothing. So, I stood there shaking this green leafy pom-pom at the scanner until I noticed that the ribbon that holds the bundle together looks an awful lot like a barcode to someone who is not wearing his reading glasses.

After a time, I located the button marked Produce, and entered the code number for cilantro, and things got worse from there.

The Self-Checkout Display Screen read: "Please place this item to the side."

I carefully placed the cilantro on top of the register.

The Self-Checkout Display Screen read: "Cannot continue until item is bagged."

I placed the cilantro in the bag.

The screen read: "Item in bag has not been scanned."

So, I removed the cilantro from the bag, stuck it under my arm and continued with my next item.

A red light flashed over my head and the screen read: "Cannot scan until item is replaced in bag. Please wait for the attendant to assist you."

I cursed and waited for the attendant.

The attendant came and pressed a few buttons, and one minute later I crashed the machine again. I looked around to see if I was being filmed, as this would be exactly the kind of gag that would make a great bit on Candid Camera.

The attendant came over, and –you guessed it– I screwed it up again. Only this time the display screen read: "Not only is your wife not going to give you that kiss you were hoping for, but when you do finally arrive home, she's really going to be hacked-off that you weren't there 20 minutes ago." Okay, I'm kidding about the last part, but I knew it was true.

I was late.

Next time, I think I'll ask her: How about if I do the cooking and you go to the store? If she would do that, I would definitely give her a big kiss when she got back and maybe run her a hot bath to boot.

Have a Sloppy Father's Day

—●●●—

Fatherhood, in real life, is messier and sloppier than those greeting cards portray.

It's not all smiles and hugs shot through an opaque lens that make fatherhood seem like just one perfectly rich and wonderfully rewarding experience after another.

No, the real fatherhood, for me at least, is about the nitty-gritty stuff like rolling up an area rug and tossing it out the 2nd story bedroom window at 3 A.M. because your child has been violently ill all over it –and you figure 'what the hell,' it only cost $19.95 from Home Depot and I'd easily rather pay another twenty bucks for a new rug than spend the next hour scrubbing the bile colored stains out of this one, only for my wife to say a week later, "It still smells like vomit in here."

It's about driving 800 miles during the week for business only to wake up on Saturday morning, get back in the car, and drive your daughter to Charlotte for a soccer tournament.

Being a dad is about keeping your mouth shut even when your oldest irons and straightens the most beautiful curly brown locks of hair you've ever seen (although secretly, I'm not above putting it in print while she's away at summer camp).

It's about listening even when you are too tired to listen, especially when the story is endless and seemingly going nowhere as in: "Hey Dad. Guess what? You know Shelly in my class, who used to sit next to Morgan, but now sits next to Brianna? Well guess what? Guess where she sits now? The teacher moved her to sit next to Kayla, who used to sit next to Olivia. But guess what? She didn't like sitting next to Kayla and so she asked the teacher if she could move and guess what the teacher said?" You listen because you know: To her, this is important stuff.

Being a dad is about making mistakes, sometimes big ones, like losing your temper and slamming your fist down on the dining room table so hard and loud it makes your six-year-old shake and cry with fear.

Being a dad means trying to remember your rising 8th grader doesn't think the old 'pull my finger' joke is so funny anymore.

Being a dad is about loving her now more than ever but still profoundly missing that stick legged, pig-tailed little girl in the photograph with a Band-Aid on her knee and knowing that she will never be that little again.

Being a dad is about knowing middle-school girls can be really mean and cruel to each other.

Being a dad is about still urging your youngest to give that elderly aunt a kiss even when you can still remember from your own childhood Aunt Elsie's fleshy jowls and protruding lips as she said, "Come hear and give me some sugar."

Being a dad is about hearing, "Hey Dad, watch this," or "Hey Dad, look at me," over and over and over and still trying your hardest to remain interested after the twentieth time.

So for me, being a dad, so far, has been a long, worrisome, sloppy, mistake filled, exhausting experience mixed in with –I must confess– some wonderful moments of complete joy, absolute delight, and utter happiness.

These sort of things are hard to put into a Hallmark card, but dads out there know what I'm talking about. So, to all the fathers out there, from one dad to another, have a sloppy and imperfect Father's Day.

Yard Work Is a Battle

———•••———

I know some people who think of yardwork as being peaceful and relaxing. Not me. I think of it as all out warfare.

Every summer the honeysuckle amasses arms; the dandelions launch sneak attacks by dropping tiny white paratroopers into my yard. The ivy shamelessly crosses over its borders, while the clover quietly commences a full-scale invasion.

For 16 years, I've battled my lawn.

Sometimes it feels like I'm a winner; other times a looser.

If you have a plot of grass of any size, I'm guessing you know what I mean?

But thanks to various chemical weapons like Weed-B Gone, I've been –for the most part– able to keep these weed-insurgencies in check. At least I was able, until a newcomer arrived on the scene: a weed so big and bad that it has almost completely choked out all the grass that I've lovingly fought to preserve for all these years.

You see, our yard has become a breeding ground for crabgrass. And to make matters worse, I've apparently been mowing over it for sometime now and not really realizing what it was.

In truth, I thought it was a different type of grass that maybe had spread from the backyard to the front. (We have all kinds of weird stuff growing in the back.) But it wasn't until my wife remarked on it that I really took notice. "What is this weird curly grass that's all over the place?" she asked.

When I said I didn't know, we decided to look it up online.

A few minutes later I had an image up on my daughter's I-Pad. "This is it," I said, showing her a picture on the screen of exactly what was growing all over our yard.

"That looks exactly like what we've got," she agreed. "It says here that one single crabgrass plant can spread 150,000 seeds at a time."

I kept reading, "It says, '...if you have crabgrass you should mow with the bag attachment and wash the blades of your mower afterward....but that will just slow the spreading."

I also learned that in a fight between crabgrass and Chuck Norris....crabgrass wins.

I made that last one up, but you get the idea.

As I read further, the gravity of the situation began to sink in. All of our back yard and about half the front was blanketed in the stuff.

"It's apparently very hard to get rid of. This website recommends pulling it out by hand, or spraying defoliant on the entire yard. And it says the crabgrass will choke out all the grass and the yard will be completely covered in crabgrass if we don't."

"You're kidding," I said swallowing hard and thinking back to just five minutes ago, when I was happy and unaware that my lawn had reached terminal status.

Sometimes I hate the internet.

With a sickening feeling in my stomach, I stood up and began walking out of the room.

"Where are you going?" Michele asked.

"I'm going up to the laundry room to see if I can find an old pillow case or something. I need to make a white flag, because I'm seriously thinking about surrendering."

Big Fat Presbyterian Wedding

———•••———

"You act like you don't even want to buy this suit," the salesman helping me joked, and, in truth, he was exactly right. I didn't want to buy this suit or any other suit and my attitude must have showed.

I was buying it for a family wedding that was coming up soon.

Now, I've always heard the number of bridesmaids is the yardstick used to measure the elaborateness of Southern weddings. This one was to have eleven. A big number, but we're not done yet. Add two junior bridesmaids, two flower girls, and that's a total of 14 standing up there in matching gowns —not including the bride. Add the groomsmen, throw in a Scottish bagpiper in kilt, and yes, it's going to be a Big Fat Presbyterian Wedding.

My mother is stoked. Nobody, not even the bride herself, is more revved up about the wedding than she is. I'm sure on some level, she is genuinely excited for the bride and groom, but I secretly suspect the real reason for her fervor is that she is looking forward to showing off her granddaughters. "The Angels," as she calls them, are to be junior bridesmaids and a flower girl.

My mother has been feverishly working with them in preparation, trying on dresses, shoes, and different hairstyles for months. She is taking no chances; her Angels will be looking their best when the big day comes.

As for the children, they would rather eat vegetables and go to bed early than be fitted for dresses. I, in turn, am encouraging them to be extra cooperative. (The term 'extra cooperative' is my polite way to tell the kids to shut-up and quit complaining.)

When she finished outfitting the children, my mother unexpectedly turned her attention to me and my attire. She suggested I buy a new suit for the wedding. I felt that I didn't need one, and said so. She insisted, even offered to pay. The harder she pushed; the more stubborn I became. Eventually, my wife convinced me that I was acting more childish than the children. My wife was urging me to be extra cooperative –which is her way of saying: shut up, quit complaining and just go buy a suit.

While in Atlanta on business, I went out suit shopping. My first stop was at Neiman Marcus. I decided to look over the neckties and found one that was really nice looking. I held it up and appraisingly looked at it. Wow, I thought, this tie is beautiful. Okay if the price is not too much, I'll splurge.

I flipped it over to read the tag. You've got to be kidding. This tie must contain plutonium thread. It cost $340.

I wanted to drop it and run away as if it really was radioactive, but I kept my composure, as if I shopped for $340 ties all the time. I discreetly tucked the tie back into its place on the display table to join its other extravagantly priced friends. I must confess, after the tie experience, I didn't have the courage to even look at Neiman's suits.

I made a few more stops and wound up at a much less expensive store where I bought the suit from the salesman who accused me of not wanting it. (Oddly, the suit was only slightly more expensive than the tie at Neiman's.)

So, on the wedding day there will be 14 women all standing up there in front of the church in full regalia, a matching number of groomsmen, 300 or so invited guests, a bagpiper in kilt, and me in my new suit.

My only question is: With all that going on, who is even going to notice or even care whether my suit is new or old? The only person I can think of is my mother, but I won't say a thing.

I'm being extra cooperative.

Homeless in High Point

——●●●——

Last Friday morning, my Jeep was muscling its way through the snow with all 4 wheels pulling me along. Despite the icy slush, I was rushing to the office. I had a customer meeting and my mind was occupied with thoughts of orders and shipments.

Stopped at the light on the corner of Russell and Hamilton, a man gestured for me to roll down my window. I did. He asked if he could have a ride to the home-less shelter on Centennial. Maybe it was because of the way he was shifting his weight from foot to foot in the melting snow or maybe it was something about the way he asked – don't know exactly what– but on impulse, I said, "Get in."

The man dropped the paper cup he was holding on the ground and, nearly run-ning, made his way into my passenger's seat with snow falling from his boots and pants onto my floor mat. Right away, he cupped his hands and placed each over my heating vents.

I got a closer look at his face and realized that I knew him. I said, "Your name is Richard isn't it?"

He gave me a look of surprise, shocked that I would know his name. I gave him my name, and then, he recognized me too. We were on the same wrestling team at High Point Central.

"You remember Coach Smith?" I asked.

Richard laughed.

As we talked further, he explained that he had been laid off and his benefits had run out. The night before he had slept in at motel in Archdale and had walked in the snow from there into High Point on his way to the shelter. His roommate for the night also homeless- had stolen his jacket. When he finished his story, he let his head dip and cast his eyes on the floorboard of my car. That's when he said it. The words that would later make me cry like a two-year-old who has lost his mother.

He said, "Man Mac, I hate for you to see me like this."

It broke my heart.

As I let him out I said, "Richard I want to help you.

Having no clue how to reach him or contact him, I wrote the address of my church on the back of a magazine. I said, "I don't know yet what I'll have there for you, but I'll have something."

He said, "Thanks."

As he shut the door, I shut my eyes and cried. His remark, "I hate for you to see me like this," really got to me.

The first person I thought to call was Thom Stout, a close friend since childhood, and who, incidentally, was on the same wrestling team. After telling him the story, we went together on a shopping spree at K-Mart. Having never done this sort of thing before, we fumbled our way through the men's section buying this and that and guessing at sizes. We settled on several necessity items, a duffle bag to put it all in, and included a gift card as well. Thom also said that he had an opening in the packing department in his factory.

From there I drove to the church and left our package with the job information for him to pick up.

I live a comfortable life. My biggest worries are about work -how I'm going to find the time to get it all done- and of course I worry about my wife and children and their welfare. My worries seem so trifling compared to not having a place to call home.

Honestly, I've troubled myself more about how far the Panthers will advance in the playoffs than I have worried about the plight of the unsheltered. However, in the few days since my ride with Richard, my perspective has started to change.

As a start, I called Steve Key, the director of Open Door Ministries and asked what kind of assistance the shelter needs. Steve told me they need volunteers, in the form of: churches, other organizations or individuals to prepare and serve meals. They are seeking donations of personal items such as toiletries, towels and washcloths or if you wish to contribute funds; send to: Open Door Ministries, P.O. Box 1528, High Point, NC 26261. The telephone number is 336-885-0191.

I have decided to donate the proceeds of this column to the Open Door Ministries –in honor of a teammate.

What Exactly is Awapuhi?

——•••——

TEENAGER'S BATHROOM -Unable to use his own bathroom after a recent re-caulking job, area resident, Mac Lane, was stunned to find a veritable hoard of high-end bath gels, designer soaps and scientifically formulated shampoos in the shower used by his teenage daughters.

"It's like a whole different world in there," the balding, 175lb, father of three was quoted as saying, "I've never seen so much soapy stuff in all my life."

Among the dazzling display of items discovered by Lane was: a tube of foaming face wash; several bottles of scented body scrub; a container of frizz-ease; hydrating, organic and weatherizing shampoos; deep moisturizing body washes; skin cleansers; de-tanglers; hair conditioners; various styles of shavers; some sort of pouf scrubbing device; a mysterious product made from coral reef extract; and something called Jojoba.

Lane, who normally depends on basic Dial soap and Suave shampoo for his bathing needs, was initially confused by the vast array of designer cleansing products. Among his uncertainties: What is Awapuhi and will it really help to recapture my skins youthful glow in just five days? What does the ancient Hawaiian god Kanaloa have to do with shampoo? Does my face lack SilkiEssence™? How does one measure 75% smoother hair? And just where do I put this Jojoba stuff?

At one point in the showering process, Lane reportedly dabbed a small amount of scientifically formulated hydrating skin gel with mirco-infused peppermint oils and spread it onto his chest and armpits.

Lane then combined the Oil of Olay Organic Cleanser with John Frieda's Weatherizing Skin Hydrating Formula to create a frothy goo which reportedly took several minutes of rinsing to remove from his hands.

Experimenting further, Lane sampled the Naked Naturals Awapuhi and Lavender shampoo, the Jojoba gel and rinse, and reportedly applied a small amount of the Frizz-Ease into the few remaining hairs atop his head.

"I must have the cleanest and most pampered daughters in town," Lane admitted Wednesday. "It took me twenty minutes just to read the labels on all this stuff."

Of further concern to Lane was, "Who exactly is paying for all this fancy stuff that smells like a flower shop?"

"I wouldn't exactly rank Australian Maximum Hydrating Tea Tree Oil Conditioner or Radiant Ribbons of Deep Lavender Moisturizing Body Cleanser as necessity items," Lane said. "I don't want to sound too much like a cheapskate, but I do think we could save a bunch of money by purchasing more basic soaps and shampoos from now on."

"It looks to me like, there's a lot of money going down the drain in our house."

Lane's teenage daughters were unavailable for comment before going to press.

The Nature Boy is Still Wrestling?

—●●●—

While staying in a hotel the other night, I chanced upon one of those Wrestling Smack-Down shows where everyone –the wrestlers, the managers, the wrestler's girlfriend, even the manager's girlfriend– eventually ends up outside the ring in a big melee, beating the crap out of one another and bashing each other about the head with metal folding chairs.

Only this particular Smack-Down was different because, right there in the center ring, bleached blond hair and all, stood none other than Ric Flair, The Nature Boy himself. He was dressed in shirt sleeves and tie (I think they do this so it will appear unscripted) in the ring and shouting threats at someone-or-other.

I stood, mouth agape in front of the television, unable to believe my eyes.

Perhaps a little background is in order, as to why this amazed me so. You see, I used to pretend to be Ric Flair. Let me repeat that for a little added emphasis: as a child, I used to pretend to be Ric Flair.

Back in the mid 1970's, when I was 6 or 7 years old, my cousin Will and I went through this huge professional wrestling phase.

Will would dress up in a black ski mask and I would don a cape (actually a bath towel safety pinned around my neck) and we would launch ourselves like demons off the top rope (the sofa), dropping Atomic Elbows onto each other.

We spent many a happy Saturday afternoon blissfully head-butting, body slamming, and head locking each other just like the real TV wrestlers.

We had a whole routine choreographed, and judging by the accounts of our relatives who watched us perform, we were pretty good. (I can remember the hardest part of the act was trying to pretend to be asleep -and not giggle- when Will slapped me in the dreaded "Sleeper" hold.)

As our enthusiasm grew, Will and I begged our fathers to take us to see the actual matches themselves. Live.

I personally saw the likes of Andre the Giant in a cage match vs. Black Jack Mulligan (this is way before Hulk Hogan came on the scene). I saw Rufus R. Jones, also known as 'The Freight Train,' in title bout vs. Wahoo McDaniel as well as tag team matches with Arn and Oli Anderson, Dusty Rhodes, a Polynesian Giant named Tio Tio, and of course The Nature Boy himself Ric Flair.

This is why I was so stunned to see old Ric still in the ring. That was 40 years ago.

"Ric Flair must be 100 years old," I wondered aloud. "Could this be some sort of weird Pro-Wrestling Senior Tour?"

I'm 45 years old and I was learning my multiplication tables when I first saw Ric Flair perform.

In the time since then, I've had one wife, two career changes, three children, four mortgages, and five U.S. presidents. I've completed elementary school, middle school, high school and graduated from College and, incredibly, there's old Ric still out there in the ring.

As I stood in the hotel room gaping at the screen, I thought about perhaps calling Will and challenging him to a rematch. I wondered how silly we would look if we revived the old wrestling routine with the ski mask, bath-towel cape and all.

Pretty ridiculous huh? Still, it might be fun. (I'll bet I could hold my giggles better now.)

I have to admit, for a man easily old enough to be a grandfather, the aged Nature Boy didn't look too bad out there and, in spite of myself, I found myself rooting for him once again.

And I couldn't help but think, maybe the secret to longevity is getting repeatedly hit over the head with a metal folding chair.

Look at Me Dad!

————•••————

It took a family beach trip over Father's Day weekend to finally figure out the answer to a question I've been wrestling with for years: What is the most important part of being a dad?

Is it to be a teacher? A decision maker? Disciplinarian? Coach? Breadwinner? Listener? Lecturer?

My insight into this fatherhood conundrum came at Alligator Adventure of all places, a tourist trap of king-sized proportions located in North Myrtle Beach, South Carolina.

With my kids trailing along behind me past various reptile exhibits, I came upon another dad. Even before I saw his kids, who were apparently somewhere in the distance behind him as well, I recognized him for who he was. This guy was a dad just like me. I could tell by the wrinkled Penn State T-shirt he wore, the loose-fitting khaki shorts, the camera hanging about his neck, and, of course, the fanny pack.

His kids shouted from somewhere behind him, "Look Daddy! Ooooh. They're feeding them!"

Upon hearing this, my kids shot ahead to see what all the fuss was about. An instant later they started to beseech me in the same manner, "Oh wow! Come over here Dad, look at this!"

As we both stood there in the heat with our kids, the Penn State Dad and I obediently watched Utan the Colossal Crocodile chomp down bits of chicken parts. At one point, Penn State gave me a nod that was sort of an I-really-am-enjoying-this-but-I'm-trying-to-play-this-cool-and-can't-really-act-like-I'm-enjoying-this-as-much-as-I-am sort of a look. I nodded back in much the same way; I understood.

I wondered, how many times on this Myrtle Beach vacation have I heard, "Watch this Dad" -like when my oldest stood up on the surfboard and rode in on a wave. Or "Look at me Dad" when my middle daughter brushed her hair aside to reveal two newly pierced ears her mother had taken her to get that morning. Or "Look at this Dad," when my youngest girl found a seashell in the sand.

This is when I had my epiphany.

Like most really hard questions we ask ourselves in life, the obvious answer is often surprisingly easy. I realized the most important part of a being a father is simply to be wherever your kids are and look at whatever it is they show you. That's it. Just look and remark to let them know you are interested. Let them know you approve, let them know you think they're beautiful, or let them know you think they are the greatest.

My kids can't get enough of this, and, if I'm being really honest, I can't either. God has blessed me with a wonderful and loving dad and even though I'm an adult now, I still love to share my successes with my father. The words I use are more grown-up, of course, but the message is still the same: "Look at me Dad."

Harry Potter Madness

———•••———

Driving back from a business meeting in Hickory late on Friday afternoon, my cell phone chirped. It was my wife, Michele. "We're going to Barnes and Noble to get in line for the new Harry Potter book."

My 11-year-old, Cannon, has been counting the days for months.

About 10 minutes later another chirp sounded. "You can't believe how many people are here! There must be 400 people in this line."

"To buy the book?" I asked dumbly.

"No, not to buy the book. To get a wrist band to buy the book," Michele said using a tone of voice that reminded me of the way a teacher might sound when addressing a clueless student. "The book doesn't go on sale until midnight."

Another chirp about an hour later, "We got a wrist band. We're in the blue group."

"That's great."

"No....that's not great. That's terrible." She said, again with the cluless student voice. "Blue is the last group. The gold group goes first. Then red, then green, then orange, then silver, then yellow, then purple, and then finally blue. We're in the last group because we didn't pre-order...anyway...when will you be home? They're having a Potter Party that starts at 8:30."

I had a grueling work week and the last thing I wanted to do was go to a Harry Potter Party at Barnes and Noble. I decided to use our 6-year-old as my excuse. "That sounds kind of late for Anna. Why don't I stay home and put her to bed?"

"Oh come on," My wife cajoled. "It'll be fun. Most of the kids are dressing up and lots of adults are in costume too."

After dinner, my 11-year-old put on one of my neckties, fixed her hair and pronounced herself Harry's faithful friend Hermione Granger. My six-year-old, Anna, who incidentally, reads on a "see spot run" level and who doesn't know the wizard Harry Potter from M.A.S.H.'s Colonel Potter, decided she wanted to dress up too.

"I've got a great idea for Anna's costume," my 11 year old declared. "Let's take one of dad's old t-shirts and cut it up to look ragged. Then we'll smear it with dirt, give her a pair of mismatched socks and she can go as Dobby the House Elf."

I vaguely remembered from the book that House Elves like to wear, in fact treasure, old, discarded clothing. I nodded agreement and suggested she use crayons and markers to make the shirt appear soiled rather than using actual dirt.

The kids worked together and in about three minutes Anna's Dobby the House Elf costume was complete and we were in the car.

Once inside the store, it was like some strange medieval circus —no that's not exactly accurate— it was more like Trekies gone Wizard for New Year's Eve.

Of the children, Hermiones and bespectacled Harrys were by far the popular get-ups, and among the adults (yes, there were lots of folks old enough to have graduated from Hogwarts some time ago in costume) we spotted two white haired Lucious Malfoys, four Dumbledores, a Narcissa, and two Professor McGonagalls.

My wife trotted Anna over to enter the costume contest in her slapdash ragged t-shirt with mismatched socks. This was the main event and there were so many kids, the contest was to be staged in five heats.

Our little House Elf, remarkably won her heat and advanced to the finals. When her turn came in the last round, she tousled her hair (to make it look messy as coached by big sis) and stepped onto the platform. As the judge announced her name, Anna shrugged her shoulders and gave the crowd an 'aw-shucks' smile that was somehow both adorable and bashful at the same time.

Well, that did it. The crowd erupted with claps and cheers for the little House Elf Anna in her big sister's three-minute costume as she won the first prize.

The staff at Barnes and Noble graciously let Anna and I leave for home while Mom and big sister stayed to claim the grand prize of buying the first Harry Potter book sold at the stroke of midnight.

I hope on this bizarre night my kids learned that teamwork can sometimes take the form of a ripped t-shirt, a pair of mismatched socks and tousled hair.

I know I learned that sometimes it's better to go ahead and go to whatever it is, no matter how outlandish it may seem at first.

Santa Claus Rocks the Lane House

———•••———

'Twas the week after Christmas and in the Lane home,
I heard strange music coming from the living room.

This tune was quite different. It was a curious song…
Definitely not the Hip Hop my daughters play all day long.

My girls like rappers who drive big fancy cars;
and who sing about going out to da-clubs and da-bars.

But this strange new tune was no electronic re-mix,
it was music I liked, with real guitar licks.

As I drew closer, I recognized the refrain.
Could that be Foghat? No, I must be insane.

No way. No how. I thought, this just couldn't be.
Wasn't their last hit back in 1973?

But sure enough, "Slow Ride" was the song I was hearing,
and my three daughters loved it, in fact they were cheering.

Have these kids gone mad? Are they musically deranged?
So what has caused such a drastic change?

I think Santa himself caused this transformation,
and he alone is responsible for this musical education.

His gift to our girls was an electronic Wii game,
and the songs in our house may never be the same.

The girls' favorite game is "Guitar Hero" by far,
and to win one must become a Rock Star.

With a miniature guitar, the player will strum,
as the notes on the screen show the rhythm.

The goal is to jam like Hendrix, Clapton or Page,
if you do well in the game, you light up the stage.

You get extra points if you twirl and groove,
and rip the guitar like Townsend of Who.

This strange little game, so tiny and small,
has unleashed for the kids a Rock free-for-all.

My girls play ZZ Top, Santana, The Stones,
Guns and Roses, Kiss, and even The Ramones.

Now I'm not as old as Handel, or Bach,
I just like good ole classic rock.

But for them, this Rock and Roll is novel and new,
and it's the music I like and they love it too.

Maybe this Wii game has given some appreciation,
for the music that came from my generation.

Before Santa's gift, my kids thought me "old school,"
but I think now they've learned...Dad's music is cool.

So if you drive by my house and hear an electric guitar a wailin'
just know the Lane girls are rockin' like Eddie Van Halen.

Emails From The Dead

———•••———

04-12-09
TO: MOMMABEAR334@EMAIL.COM
FROM: MARYBETH14@EMAIL.COM

Hi Mom, We are in Atlanta, Georgia, and as I'm writing this, a guy is passed-out on the hood of our car. There are like a jillion really freaky-looking people in this parking lot and the concert ended like two hours ago.

I know you said I should try and spend more time with Dad and Spring Break would be a great time to do that....but honestly Mom....I'm beginning to think The Grateful Dead Reunion Tour was not the best idea????

Dad played his boot-legs the entire way. It sucked. I must have heard three decades worth of Truckin' on the way here.

The only cool thing that's happened is that Dad bought me a tie-dye, but then he totally nerded out. He walked up to this guy and his daughter who were selling these giant pink balloons. I was like, "Dad, I'm fourteen...not four. I don't do balloons anymore." But guess what? He bought the balloon anyway and he spent the next thirty minutes breathing all the air out of it himself. His face turned red, and the only thing he could say for the next two hours was to mumble the words "Killer" over and over.

I love you, Mary Beth

04-14-09
TO: MOMMABEAR334@EMAIL.COM
FROM: MARYBETH14@EMAIL.COM

Hi Mom, We are in Washington, DC, and Dad is like totally freaking out. I know you said for me to try and enjoy this little adventure, but he keeps pumping his fists in the air and shouting, "Was that amazing or what?"

He bought two more of those balloons before the concert. I've never seen him act like this.

Love, Mary Beth

04-15-09
TO: MOMMABEAR334@EMAIL.COM
FROM: MARYBETH14@EMAIL.COM

Hi Mom, We are in Charlottesville, Virginia, and I just want you to know…Dad threw his cell phone into the river when we left D.C.

Love, Mary Beth

04-17-09
TO: MOMMABEAR334@EMAIL.COM
FROM: MARYBETH14@EMAIL.COM

Hi Mom, We are in Albany, NY, and Dad insisted we park next to the van with the balloons. The man who sells them is named Mr. Trips and he has a daughter, Rainfall, who's like a year older than me.

Rainfall said Dad has bought so many balloons that they're going to build an indoor lap pool when they get back to Oregon.

This trip has sucked from the beginning.

Love, Mary Beth

04-18-09
TO: MOMMABEAR334@EMAIL.COM
FROM: MARYBETH14@EMAIL.COM

Mom, We are in Worcester, MA, and Dad gave our tickets to Rainfall, left me in the car, and said he was going on a "little trip of his own." When he got back, -about four hours later!- he said, I was the most brightly-colored angel-soldier in the endless sea of the galaxy. (I'm sure he meant it to be sweet, but it came out whacked.)

Can you please come get me?

Love, Mary Beth

04-21-09
TO: MOMMABEAR334@EMAIL.COM
FROM: MARYBETH14@EMAIL.COM

Mom, We are in Buffalo, NY, and Dad said he is seriously thinking about making some "radical life-changes." He also said hanging out with Mr. Trips is ten times more fun than living with you and selling insurance back home. And he's started calling me Starlight....as if?

I think you should come get me,

Love, Mary Beth

04-22-09
TO: MOMMABEAR334@EMAIL.COM
FROM: MARYBETH14@EMAIL.COM

Mom, We are in Wilkes Barre, PA, and Dad hasn't slept or showered in the past four days.

I think you should come get me!!!

Love, Mary Beth

04-24-09
TO: MOMMABEAR334@EMAIL.COM
FROM: MARYBETH14@EMAIL.COM

Seriously Mom!! We are in Hartford, CT, and Dad says we are totally out of money. He wants me to find someone who'll pay cash for the Acura. Me? I've never sold a car.

Please hurry!

Love, Mary Beth

04-26-09
TO: MOMMABEAR334@EMAIL.COM
FROM: MARYBETH14@EMAIL.COM

Mom, We are in Uniondale, NY, and Dad's asking everyone to call him Captain Daydream. He studies his hands while he dances. Plus, he's really, really, really starting to smell, AND…..we sold the Acura to a guy in the parking lot for a "Kind" price (which I think was the equivalent of front row seats and a bag of something) Now we are riding and sleeping in Mr. Tripps and Rainfall's van.

I AM MISERABLE!!

You really need to come and get me…LIKE NOW!!!! Just ask anyone where the "Trippin' Whippetts" van is and that's where you'll find us. Hurry!!!

Love, Starlight……..oh no! What am I saying??? Please hurry! Mary Beth

Obesity of the Menu

————•••————

When did restaurant menus become so obese with description?

Maybe it was around the same time black coffee and Sanka yielded making way for more exotic blends like cappuccinos, frappuccinos and lattes. Or when dolphin -the fish not Flipper- started appearing on menus as the more glamorous sounding mahi-mahi. Or perhaps it was about the time the word organic –a term I used to associate with fertilizer– worked its way into fashion.

I don't know when this all started, but nowadays, it seems many nice –and even some not so nice– restaurants are serving up heaping helpings of description with every meal.

Sometimes you must negotiate six, seven or even eight adjectives before you find out whether it's fish or fowl that's being served. Chicken is more likely to be offered as something like: Sautéed Free-Range Chicken Breast Topped with a Peppered Pan Sauce.

Those who know me know I'm a bit of a talker. Usually, I'm so busy running my mouth that I forget to study the menu and when the waiter approaches the table, I invariably feel the way I felt when as a kid I hadn't done my homework properly. My head goes down, my eyes dart this way and that, as I cram for the imminent menu exam.

"Appetizer?" the waiter asks.

I nervously found the section marked "appetizers." I noticed that each item was a paragraph long as I searched about.

I picked one at random. It's just an appetizer and if I don't care for it, I'll just invite everyone at the table to share mine.

"And for your main course?"

Still cramming, I was between the Grilled North Carolina, Low Country Shrimp (everyone knows these are far superior to shrimp from say Three Mile Island or Love Canal) Served Over Stone Ground Parmesan Cheese Grits or the Marinated Ashley Farms Free-Range Chicken Breast topped with Tasso Ham (which I guess is better than Taco Ham or even Torso Ham) in a Smoked Gouda Sauce.

It's as if from these elaborate descriptions the composer of the menu wants me to believe that he has personally scouted the world in search of just the right ingredients, creating the illusion that he himself ground my corn with stones in Parmesan, or that he has been out free-ranging with chicken breasts, or perhaps smoking gouda.

I got the shrimp and grits thing and it was actually pretty good.

Understand that it's not the food that I have a problem with, but rather the hoity-toity way it's presented on the menu that bugs me more than anything else. While I may not be the most cultured diner, I'm certainly not Ernest T. Bass either. I like good food, who doesn't?

In conclusion, many of you who are sophisticated epicureans might think that I may have recently cascaded from my perch atop a generously tempting pile of transported, organically-grown root vegetables. Or -in plain English- you might think I just fell off a turnip truck.

Actually, I just like to keep things simple.

Renting a Man's Home is His Hassle

——•••——

Like refugees in the path of an invading army, we grab our belongings and flee from our house –although not before putting the nice guest towels out in all the bathrooms.

Every Furniture Market we rent. And every market we swear we'll never rent again.

"This is it. This is absolutely the last time," my wife says.

"Okay, okay," I say. "We are never renting again."

Moving out a family of five twice a year is an enormous hassle, but once we are snuggled back in our own beds again and, more importantly, the proceeds are nestled in our bank account, the memories of the ordeal have a tendency to fade.

This year, market is in late April. So in about a week we'll be at it again, cleaning and cleaning and cleaning and cleaning then after we're done cleaning, we'll pay three cleaning ladies to come in and clean some more resulting in a thoroughly immaculate house that's infinitely more spic and span than it ever is when the Lanes are in residence.

Michele, my wife, packs for herself as well as for our three daughters. This is a chore because she must know which of the myriad of hairbrushes and hair products to include. These items outweigh all the essentials like pants, shoes and socks in the minds of our girls. The older two, I think, would rather go to school carrying a live rattlesnake than to leave the house with unkempt hair.

By the time the packing is finished, the car is crammed to the brim with stuff. I imagine a rocking chair lashed to the top of the mini-van as we become the High Point Hill-Billies.

We stay at my father's house in Greensboro. His house is on a golf course, but unfortunately no swimming pools, no movie stars.

We were told by someone –I forget who– to make space for the renters in our dressers and closets. I start by removing each drawer from the dresser and tipping it sideways allowing the contents to dump into a Hefty bag, which I then throw into the attic. I have perfected this operation over the years and can perform it in about 60 seconds flat.

Rummaging in the attic not long ago, I came across what at first looked like a dozen or more dehydrated elephant eggs clustered in a nest of fiberglass insulation. They were, of course, my collection of market bags that I had forgotten to retrieve upon my return.

I brought them downstairs to have a look.

I spent an hour just looking at my small pieces of my life wrapped by Hefty. Mixed in amongst the old socks was some really great stuff. There was a ticket stub from a basketball game when Dean Smith was coach. Some photographs of my girls when they were tiny. A bag of shark's teeth from a vacation at the beach, birthday cards from my wife, and artwork my young daughters had made with glitter and construction paper from a long-forgotten Sunday school class of the past.

The market bags were like miniature time capsules of my life and I had an idea to neatly sum up this column with some romantic notion of how I wouldn't have had the chance to reflect and reminiscence if not for the hassle of the moving out, but that wouldn't be altogether truthful. While I did enjoy my trip down Market Bag Lane, the reason we put ourselves through this torture twice a year is that the extra cash really comes in handy.

And, for the record, we've both decided this is absolutely the last market that we are ever renting. No really, this is it.

Really.

Gardening Failure

———•••———

It's officially autumn.

I wish I could go into lengthy descriptions of all the copious produce that our summer garden produced....but I can't.

By late July, our garden was the equivalent of a backyard Chernobyl: A complete horticultural meltdown.

The sad thing is, it began with such high hopes.

Back in late April, as a family, we dug two small plots in the yard -each about the size of a picnic table, and surrounded it with wooden rails and finials from a kit we bought from Home Depot.

We filled in the space with a mixture of topsoil and manure.

My wife and my daughters really got into it, all of us digging and hoeing, spreading and watering.

As I turned the soil, I imagined all manner of fresh veggies we'd soon be picking. I thought that perhaps, our garden might be so productive that we might even grow one of those gigantic watermelons or prize-winning pumpkins that you see in the newspaper.

But it wasn't to be.

We planted mostly seedlings from the Farmer's Market, and this quickly became our first problem. My girls found the tiny seedlings irresistibly cute, and they wanted to buy nearly everything they saw. I imagine my girls looked on those fresh green sprouts as something like helpless baby-plants that needed someone to take care of them or like the botanical equivalent of homeless puppies. They wanted to buy a tray of everything...."Can we get this Dad? Can we plant these Dad? Pleassssseeeee?"

For the record, I said no to the sweet potatoes, and no to the cantaloupes, but I crumbled like an empty bag of manure on the watermelon, cucumbers, bell pepper, crook-neck squash, basil, parsley, and zucchini.

I was pretty sure we didn't have anywhere near enough room for all the stuff we bought, but we were having a good time as a family so I figured, what the heck, we'll just cram it all in there somehow.

At first, all was well in the Lane vegetable garden. For the first few weeks, after dinner, we would inspect the progress. The kids could be counted on to water it each evening. But then a strange thing started to happen. When the temperature reached the high nineties, and the mosquitoes started to swarm, no one seemed very eager to step outside and tend to our plot.

Left untended, everything started to go wrong in our small garden patch.

The cucumbers grew over the squash; the watermelon covered the herbs; the dog dug a hole in the center of one of the plots and uprooted several plants. Then, while we were on vacation for a week in mid July, the garden became parched and dry, and by late July, there was almost nothing left but dried leaves and stalks.

Even now, in late September, most vegetable gardens in our neighborhood, still appear leafy and green and are still producing. While the only thing our dried-up garden produces are looks of pity from our neighbors, who have to look at what a mess we've made.

All told, I think we harvested three squash, one zucchini, one grossly undersized watermelon about the size of softball, and about ten cucumbers.

But we did have fun, and the seedlings were cute.

I wonder if they give blue ribbons for the smallest, most undersized watermelon?

Repairs

———•••———

I want to make this very clear. I am not good at anything mechanical, even at the most basic level.

As embarrassing as this is to admit, I once drilled about 30 or so holes in the ceiling of my porch while searching for a joist in which to hang a swing.

I think in the beginning, I was hoping I'd drill one, possibly two holes and that by some great stroke of luck, I'd find the joist. Well....I didn't get lucky. I drilled the first hole, then another, and so on until saw dust -or more accurately drill dust- fell into my eyes causing me to lose my balance and fall sideways off the ladder. Note– any fall from a ladder is bad, but try doing it sometime with both eyes closed.

Bruised but resolute, I climbed back up the ladder and resumed my joist hunting adventure. Still no luck. I'd drilled about 30 holes when I finally realized the absurdity of what I was doing.

My ceiling had more holes than a Putt-Putt golf course and I only had myself to blame. In shame, I showed my wife, Michele, the mess I'd made. She pursed her lips in an expression which I took to mean how-could-I-have-married-such-a-complete-buffoon, and she said after a beat, "I'll call Kimberly."

Michele's friend Kimberly is a licensed contractor. I'm sure she could hang a porch swing in less time than it would take me to fall off the ladder....again.

By the end of the day, the swing was hung perfectly. I can't remember exactly but it seems Kimberly was on a job site somewhere driving a bulldozer or putting a new roof on a skyscraper or doing something equally impressive, so she asked her husband Roger to do the job. Roger hung the swing expertly, and to his credit, didn't remark on the holey mess I'd made of my ceiling.

The reason I mention this is to say that lately I've been dabbling in car repair if you can believe it, and I've actually surprised myself with what I good job I've been doing.

Even my wife who's had to endure many, many of my home repair related catastrophes has been impressed with my new-found expertise, and I have to give all the credit to YouTube.

This started when my old college roommate told me about how he fixed his washing machine by ordering the part on-line and how he watched YouTube and learned to make the repair. He told me that he'd starting fixing his car that way as well.

I've got two kids in college. Both have cars. Plus my car and my wife's car... needless to say, we have lots of little things that need fixing. So rather than go broke, I decided to go to YouTube.

My first repair was to replace a rearview mirror on our Jeep Grand Cherokee. I typed in "2007 Jeep Grand Cherokee mirror replacement" and sure enough, there was a video of a mechanic showing me exactly how to make the repair. With a feeling of some trepidation, I ordered the part on-line. I said a short prayer that I wouldn't make a total mess out of this job too; I watched and re-watched the video several times to be certain I knew what to do. Well, I'm happy to report that I followed the steps exactly and in about 15 minutes, voila, I had replaced the mirror myself. Perfectly.

Since then, I've replaced a turn signal relay by removing and replacing the dash board in my daughter's car. I've ordered and programed keys myself, I've recharged my own air conditioning, and most recently crawled under the car and tightened the emergency brake cable, all because of YouTube.

I have to admit, that while I'm not ready to replace a transmission yet, these small repairs have been kind'a fun.

And the best part is what my wife said, just yesterday, "I think you should go for it. You're getting good at making repairs."

I think maybe she's forgotten about the whole porch swing thing...so let's don't

remind her.

School Projects

———•••———

Let's forget about the students for a minute…school projects are downright tricky for parents.

The hardest part is to help your kid, without helping too much.

With three daughters ages 19, 16 and 11, I've helped with my share of school

projects. But as I've said, it's hard to know how much to help.

I've learned there are some parents who definitely go over-board.

I know. It's easy to do. There is a fine line between "I think you should put the glue here" and "Oh here, just give me the glue, or better yet…let me go get my wood carving tools and I'll carve you a scale model of the Taj Mahal and you can glue it onto the poster board."

And on the other extreme, I'm sure there must be a parent out there… somewhere out there…who has never helped his or her kid at all.

If so, I've never met those parents.

It's been my experience that most parents help, and help more than just a little bit. A scale model of the Eiffel tower? A diorama of the Battle of the Bulge? A working nuclear reactor brought in by a fifth grader?

What brought this to mind is that last week, Anna, my 5th grader, was sitting in the passenger's seat with her school project balanced delicately on her knees. I winced at each little bump in the road and couldn't help glancing over to see if any of the trees had fallen over.

The trees were my contribution.

"You sure you don't want me to help you carry it inside?" I asked.

"No dad. I'm okay."

"You go in the same door as the high school kids," I said. "I'd hate for you to get bumped and drop your project."

This is what I said, but I also had another reason for wanting to help her carry it in. I wanted to eyeball the other projects. I wanted to see how my daughter's stacked up against the competition.

"I can open the doors for you."

"I got it Dad."

The assignment was to read a non-fiction book and to construct a visual. When I came home from work the day before, I found that my daughter had already made a life-size Leopard Gecko out of modeling clay. Her plan was to let it dry during dinner and paint it later in the evening. She was planning to fill the top of a J. Crew shirt box with sand and rocks to make a desert scene and place the painted clay gecko inside.

I held the flashlight as she collected sand and rocks from the back yard, and I couldn't help myself. "Anna," I said. "Let's clip some of this rosemary. It might make good trees."

Rosemary clippings, as it turns out, make excellent trees when pressed into a small ball of clay to help them stand upright.

When my daughter got home that night, I asked her, "So how did your project look compared to the other kids'?"

"Some of the projects were amazing," she said, and she described how amazing each was.

"Did it look like the parents helped a lot?"

After some thought she said, "Yeah."

I thought to myself: Don't these parents know? The best school projects are the ones that look good, but not too good.

Frosty's Tree

———•••———

High Point lost its most beloved tree in this past ice storm.

Frosty and Catharine Culp's 95 foot Dawn Redwood – which stood on the corner of Woodbrook and Farris in the Emerywood neighborhood of High Point for 55 years and which delighted so many at Christmas time- is no longer standing.

I spoke to Catharine first, then later her husband, Frosty about the loss of their tree and asked them to tell me again the story of how it came to be so special to so many.

"Frosty had this idea," Catharine said. "Our son, Will, who was age 11 at the time, had just had an operation to remove a bone tumor from his leg…and Frosty's idea was to decorate the big tree in the front yard with lights as a thank you to God."

"Our son, Will, had a class 1 Osteosarcoma in his leg," Frosty said. "The surgery was a success and Will never had chemo. That Christmas, the Christmas after the operation I wanted to light the tree as a dedication to the power and glory of God. I'm getting a little choked up as I'm talking about this, but we've lit the tree every year since Will's surgery and he's 33 years old now and a father himself."

"Frosty called an electrician to help him hang the lights," Catharine said. "The electrician had his daughter on his shoulders helping him hang the lights. At first I thought it was going to look terrible, but when he turned it on, it was perfect."

"That tree has become so special to so many people," Catharine said. "We've had requests over the years to light the tree for births and deaths. So many people loved that tree."

I asked if the tree had a name and Frosty said they called it "The Hope Tree."

I had first heard the story of the Culp's Hope Tree in a Christmas sermon given by Dr. Charles (Chuck) Wilson, who was then the pastor of Wesley Memorial United

Methodist Church. Chuck, as he likes to be called, told about Will Culp's surgery and how his parents have lit the tree every year as a testament to God's grace. Chuck also said that the Culp's recommended viewing the tree from directly underneath. Chuck said the Culps didn't mind, in fact, they encouraged folks to get out and walk up into their yard and stand under the tree.

That night, we took them up on it. There was a small crowd already there, mostly others who had heard Chuck's sermon. My wife, my three daughters and I stood under the tree. The view was breathtakingly beautiful. Looking straight up into the limbs of a 95 foot tall tree covered in colored lights against the backdrop of dark sky was simply magnificent. And we, along with many other families in High Point, have this as a part of our family's Christmas tradition every year.

Speaking about the ice storm damage to the tree, Frosty said, "I had three tree experts come look at it, to see if there was anything that we could do."

Sadly, all that's there now is a large stump where The Hope Tree once stood.

Frosty did tell me that he already has another Dawn Redwood on order. "I don't even know what it's going to cost me yet, but I went ahead and ordered another one. It's going to be about 35 feet tall."

Catharine said, "We saved some of the wood. I'd like to see if I could find an artist who could perhaps make something out of it that we could remember it by."

Topless Running

———•••———

"It's nudity," my wife, Michele, said.

"I don't think it is nudity," I responded, palms upturned. "Nudity to me is running around completely naked. I'm not like the guy in the Ray Stevens song. I'm not The Streak. I wear shorts….and a Camel Back when I run."

"But you don't wear a shirt."

And she is correct. When the thermometer gets over 80, I shuck the shirt. Not out of any vanity, mind you, but just simply in an effort to keep cool. I often go for long distances and a few degrees here and there helps.

What sparked this debate about male-shirtless-nudity was a visit from a long-time friend Ashton Blackman, who happens to be our Produce Box delivery person. I also have to mention, one of the things I like most about Ashton is that I never know exactly what she's going to say, and today, she didn't disappoint.

After she dropped off our weekly box of vegetables and upon leaving, Ashton said, "Hey Mac. I saw on Facebook that you were running topless last night."

"I haven't seen that," I said, surprised.

"Oh it's there," she said smiling.

I confessed that I was running without my shirt last night, but I had no idea my nocturnal exercises had made it onto Facebook.

"Well," Ashton said. "I've seen you jogging around before without your shirt on, and I don't think there is anything wrong with it, but it is a bit….shocking."

Did she just say shocking?

Shocking good? Or shocking bad? I didn't know. And upon reflection, and judging from the general appearance of my unclothed, untanned and underdeveloped upper torso, I feared the worst.

"Honestly, when I run, all I'm thinking about is how hot it is," I responded a bit sheepishly.

As Ashton was driving away, I turned to Michele and asked, "Is my jogging without wearing a shirt really shocking?"

This is what prompted her to make the nudity remark. "Plus," she added, "your mother thinks it's in bad taste as well."

I opened Facebook, and read the comments aloud to Michele. One said,

"Scandalous!" Another, "Shocking!" Another said, "You heathen!"

"See....." she said.

"Nobody's offended. This is all just good natured kidding," I responded.

"The fact that someone noticed you were running through Emerywood without a shirt, and posted it on Facebook proves my point."

Weakly I added, "But I go shirtless at the beach. I go shirtless at the pool."

"I still don't think it's proper," she said.

"So, let me ask you this," I asked playfully. "Is it indecent for any man to jog around the neighborhood with no shirt? Or just me?"

"I don't care about other men or what they do. I love you and I just care what you do. It's like when you go into a restaurant and the sign says 'No shoes. No shirt. No service.' It's just common decency."

I could tell that she wasn't being mean-spirited.

So, in the spirit of decency for all those whom I pass in High Point on my jogs, I have resolved to cover my torso while running in the future.

But I can't help but wonder: what if I really did decide to streak –like in the song– and jogged completely naked through town, I wonder how many hits I'd get on Facebook?

I'll bet it would also be a few degrees cooler as well.

Not So Sweet Dreams

————•••————

On Wednesday morning, still groggy from the alarm, I gently touched my wife Michele's shoulder and said, "Are you ready to get up?"

She propped herself up on one elbow, furrowed her eyebrows and said, "I dreamed I was done with you. In my dream....we were splitting up for good."

"Whoa. Hold on," I said. "We were splitting up for good? What did I do that was so bad?"

"You spit on me, that's what. You spit on me and I said this is IT. We are done Buddy. Nobody spits on me and gets away with it."

Laughing, I said, "Was this accidentally or was it deliberate?"

"Oh no. It was on purpose." She made a spraying gesture with her hands to indicate how forcefully I had apparently spit on her.

"Did this just happen out of the blue or were we in an argument or what?"

"You were riding your motorcycle over this volcano, and your tires were on fire...."

"Wait a minute," I jumped in. "I was what? Riding a motorcycle? Over a volcano? And my tires were on fire?"

"Yes," she said. "You were riding your motorcycle over this volcano like you do..." (Please note: I'm not sure why she used the phrase "like you do." I do not own a motorcycle, and even if I did, I'm pretty sure the last place I'd want to ride it would be over a flaming and active volcano.)

"And your tires were on fire," she continued. "You left flames in your tracks wherever you went. So, when you were done and you had stopped your motorcycle....

you were about to spit on the fire to put it out. I told you I thought the whole thing looked dangerous, and you said you didn't care and that's when you spit on me. You were awful."

"That is terrible," I said.

"You said you didn't care if it was dangerous or not and you spit right on me. Then I said, 'I'm done with you Buddy' and I meant it.....but then I realized I couldn't leave because you had the keys to the car."

"The car? What car?"

From her expression, it was apparent she wasn't ready to give up her anger yet.

"You know I didn't really spit on you...right?" I asked.

"Of course, I know that. I'm not crazy," she said. "But then you wanted me to be nice to some boss person you had there. You wanted me to make all nice and act like none of this ever happened. But I wouldn't do it. Nope. I refused. You had just spit on me and I wasn't going to be nice to anyone, particularly not your boss. So, I told him what a jerk you are."

I couldn't help but notice she used the present tense 'are.'

I swallowed.

"But you smoothed it over with your boss like you always do. You just smoothed it right over. But I was done with you. We were splitting up for good this time."

I noticed she switched to past tense....

So, I decided to risk a probing question. "You would be willing to sacrifice our whole marriage, the kids, the house, everything, over one spitting incident?"

"Absolutely," she said. "You ever spit on me and we are done."

I'm not really sure what the lesson to this story is, there than, to say that I've been happily married to this woman for 23 years and this is the first time I've discovered that spitting is a deal-breaker.

Like many married men, I try to make mental notes so I won't make the same mistake twice. My entry for Wednesday is as follows: Note to self; next time I'm cruising through lava on my Harley over Mt. Kilauea, please remember not to spit on Michele. Things don't go well after that.

House Snake

———•••———

Years ago, around the holiday table....it came out in conversation....that my cousin Patrick had recently purchased a pet snake.

We have a large family, and everyone wanted to know more.

"What kind of snake is it?" one cousin asked.

"It's a python." Patrick said proudly.

"How big will it get?"

"About six feet."

"What does it eat?"

"It eats mice for now...by constricting them, but when it gets bigger, it'll eat rats."

As cousin Patrick fielded more and more questions, I watched the expression on my grandmother's face. Her face showed both horror and disbelief that one of her own progeny could possess such an utterly revolting creature.

Now, my grandmother's hatred of all things snakes and snakey was legendary.

I had once watched her turn a copperhead into a bloody mess with a garden hoe in her carport.

"Where do you keep it?" another relative asked.

"It's in an aquarium at the foot of my bed," Patrick said.

This last bit of information was more than my grandmother could stomach.

She stood and pointed at Patrick, "How can you sleep at night knowing that you have a snake in your room?" She pronounced "sssnake" as if the word itself was profanity.

My aunt chimed in, readily agreeing, "I don't think I could sleep. Not if I knew there was a snake in the house."

"It can't get out," Patrick said. "The top's bolted on."

"I don't care. Just the thought of having a snake in the house. I don't know how I could sleep either."

"Sleep! Sleep!" not to be out done, my aunt chimed in again, "I don't think I'd feel comfortable even going inside a house where I knew there was a snake present."

"It's not venomous," Patrick added lamely. I think he knew this last remark was futile, but, I guess he felt –hopeless as it was– he had to respond in some way in the defense of his new pet.

"I couldn't even go inside a house if I knew there was a snake inside," my grandmother said ignoring his last remark.

"Neither could I. I could not enter a house if I knew there was a snake. I don't think I could even knock on the door for fear whoever, or whatever, is inside might open it," my aunt said in agreement.

My father, who had been quiet this whole time, spoke up loud enough for everyone present to hear, "Hey Patrick, how much are those snakes? I might be interested."

Then in a whisper he added, ".....might be worth it just to keep those two away."

Wrestling, I'm Glad It's Over

———•••———

Please forgive me for this brief excursion down memory lane. I'm sorry, but I just can't help myself.

The other night I went to a high school wrestling match. As I watched, the memories of my own wrestling days came flooding back like one of those dreams you don't remember, until you discover yourself in the middle of the same dream once again.

It's been some twenty years since I myself took to the mat, and the last wrestling match I saw, I participated in. So, I was curious to see if the sport had evolved any since my day.

Entering the gymnasium after such a long absence, I was happy to find the sport of wrestling exactly as I'd left it. (Wrestling apparently hasn't fallen victim to this 'billowy-baggy' clothing style you see in other sports like basketball.)

The gear is exactly as I remembered it. The shoes still looked like a ridiculous cross between ballerina slippers and Chuck Taylor high-tops, and the uniforms still remind one of a two piece swimsuit (with shoulder straps) a fashionable man from the 1920's might have worn to the seashore –only, minus the straw boater.

As I sat there on the bleachers, I recalled what an utterly humiliating experience my own wrestling career had been. If you ever heard the term "late bloomer," that was me in the extreme. I didn't start shaving regularly until I was an upper-class-man in college, and as for high school, I was undoubtedly the scrawniest, skinniest most prepubescent kid of my whole class. Being way too short for basketball, far too weak for baseball, much too slow for track, and too, too tiny for football, I chose wrestling because I knew I'd at least be competing against kids my own size.

Ironically, I won my first time out. I can still remember the nervous butterflies in my stomach as our team marched through the locker room headed for the weigh-in. Being in the lowest weight class (106 lbs and under) the coach nodded for me to step up on the scales first. I did so, wearing my entire uniform, warm-ups, headgear and all. The needle on the scale dropped like a stone, as I made weight with a margin of about 20 some pounds to spare. My opponent however, approached the scales with a worried look on his face. Before he stepped onto the device, he shed all his of his clothing. Completely naked, he next handed his spit cup over for his coach to hold (wrestlers often spit in cups all day long to shed that pesky water weight). The needle on the scale wavered for half a beat, then rose steadily upward. The referee who was overseeing this process immediately disqualified him. It took me a moment to realize what had happened. I had won my first match, and I didn't even have to break a sweat.

If only I could have gotten more forfeitures, my career might have been much more successful, but I'm afraid I didn't fare so well against opponents who actually made it past the weigh-ins. In short, my entire career as a wrestler was a disaster. I can't ever recall winning a match against an actual opponent. Imagine a young Barney Fife in tights and you've got a pretty good idea.

For some reason that I can't entirely recall, I stuck with it, even though there's nothing more humiliating in all of sports than hearing your classmates, parents and friends yelling, "Come on Mac! Get off your back," as you struggle help-lessly while squinting upward into the gymnasium lights, trying desperately to breathe, as you are about to be pinned.

Despite all this, I still recall my wrestling days with a touch of genuine fondness, and found myself getting a tad sentimental as I watched these contemporary high school kids out there competing.

My only real regret is: I wish I had gotten a few more forfeitures.

Defective Elf on the Shelf

———•••———

I think we got a defective 'Elf on the Shelf.'

The first night, our red-capped little guy moved from the staircase to the mantle, but after that, I think he may have gone on strike or something.

Day after day, and throughout most of last December, our elf stayed put, as if glued to the same spot.

My wife and I would be sleeping quietly upstairs, only to be awakened at first light by the sound of a heartbroken child sobbing, "Mommmmm! Daddddd! He didn't move......Again!"

"I think we got a lazy elf," I said after the eighth or ninth motionless day.

My daughter responded with, "The Fisher's have an Elf on the Shelf. They call him Snowball and he works just fine. They find him in a different spot every morning."

I silently cursed my neighbor Joe Fisher.

For those unfamiliar, *The Elf on a Shelf* is a Christmas storybook which comes with a toy elf. The book explains how your elf sits on the shelf silently watching all that goes on. Each night, the elf magically travels to the North Pole, delivering special messages to Santa Claus –presumably about who has been naughty and who has been nice– and returns to your house.

One can tell that the elf has traveled and returned because he comes to roost in a different spot about the house.

I blamed all this heartache on Joe Fisher. He bought an 'Elf on the Shelf' for his two daughters who, in turn, told my daughters, and that's when all our troubles started.

Last December, Joe Fisher's elf, Snowball, to the delight of his children, moved jauntily about the house every single night. His girls would wake up each morning in joyful anticipation of discovering what the impish little fellow had done this time.

One morning Joe's elf was discovered mischievously inside the refrigerator; another morning clutching a bottle of pancake syrup on the breakfast table, and still on another, he was perched above the girls' tooth brushes.

Snowball seemed to be making playful mischief at every turn, while our elf was as unresponsive as a cheese log.

Day after day. Our elf.....nothing.

I had dreams of strangling Snowball.

I didn't realize that when we brought this new elven guest into our home, how the stakes would be raised every morning of December. Each morning becoming like a miniature dry-run of Christmas itself, only in our case, if the elf didn't move like it's supposed to, it's as if Santa Claus totally passed you by. Tears follow.

But, I am happy to report: This story has a happy ending.

Either, my wife boxed up our lazy elf so well at the end of last Christmas, that she couldn't locate him this year, or the naughty little guy ran away –perhaps deciding he didn't really like the Lane family all that much. Either way, as December began, no one could locate him. So, after much discussion (I got out-voted) we decided, as a family, to buy another "Elf on the Shelf" for this Christmas season.

My youngest daughter, Anna, named the new elf, 'Mike.' And I have to say, Mike has turned out to be awesome. The first morning Mike was discovered having broken into a bag of chocolate chips. He has also been spotted taking a bubble bath in a bowl of marshmallows, and rappelling from a picture frame down to steal a cookie.

He has delighted our family, both the young and the old, and, last night, he drew mustaches on a family photo with a dry erase marker.

Mike hasn't missed a day, and so far this year, he may even be giving Snowball a run for his money.

Take that Joe Fisher.

Virginia Asks if Elf on the Shelf is Real?

———•••———

DEAR MR. LANE: I am 8 years old. Some of my friends at school are saying that the 'Elf on the Shelf' doesn't really travel to the North Pole each night in December to deliver secret messages to Santa Claus, and I'm beginning to believe them because on Wednesday, Thursday, Friday, and Saturday our 'Elf on the Shelf,' Chipper, didn't move from his spot on the bookshelf.

My father says, 'If you see it in the *NEWS & RECORD* it's so.'

Can you please tell me if my Elf on the Shelf is real?

Sincerely, VIRGINIA

Dear VIRGINIA: First, let me say that your father is a sensible man. He is correct to trust the *NEWS & RECORD*- particularly after this past election where fake news has abounded so. One must choose one's sources of information carefully, and if you read the NEWS-RECORD you can be sure your news isn't from some hapless blogger, partisan spin-doctor or even planted by the Russians for heaven's sake.

But back to your question: Yes, VIRGINIA, the Elf on the Shelf is real. Chipper exists as certainly as love and generosity and devotion exist, and as certainly as Santa Claus himself exists. To borrow a few words from the famous column written by Francis Church in 1897 to another girl named Virginia: "Alas! how dreary would be the world if there were no Santa Claus. It would be as dreary as if there were no VIRGINIAS. There would be no childlike faith then, no poetry, no romance to make tolerable this existence. We should have no enjoyment, except in sense and sight. The eternal light with which childhood fills the world would be extinguished."

As for the fact that Chipper hasn't moved for several days, all I can say is this: Try to forgive him. I'm sure he's a good elf at heart, even if he may be a little on the lazy side. After all, it could be that Chipper doesn't have anything bad to report.

And it's also helpful to keep in mind that all the elves on the shelves on all the shelves in the entire world are really not that important when compared to the birth of the Christ child —which is the real reason we celebrate Christmas.

And another thing: Be nice to your parents. Be sure to hug them and tell them how much you love them. In recent years, Christmas has gotten more complicated particularly since things like 'Elf on the Shelf' have come along. And sometimes it's hard for working moms, dads —and even elves— to keep up with everything that's goes on during this hectic season.

So, Merry Christmas VIRGINIA and Merry Christmas to all the VIRGINIAS out there who still believe!

The Worry of Wedding Expenses

———•••———

It's July 4th and I know I should probably write something noble and patriotic to commemorate this historic national holiday, but I just can't bring myself to do it.

Please don't get me wrong, my hesitancy is not because of any beef or quarrel I have with my country. I love the U.S.A. and greatly respect those who serve and protect our freedom....but I just can't bring myself to write about any of that now. You see, I've been a bit distracted –maybe panicked is a better word– ever since I spoke to a friend of mine about how much she and her husband paid for thier daughter's wedding.

In the days since, I've scarcely been able to think of anything else. I've woken up nights in a cold sweat. I've dreamed of angry knife wielding caterers chasing me through dark alleys demanding I fork over thousands of dollars for crab puffs and bacon-wrapped shrimp on those little bamboo skewers.

Plus, I've been worrying about things I never knew existed. Things like: how much does one pay for wedding dress preservation? And how much do save-the-date announcement cards cost?

I've always known that weddings are expensive, but the figures this woman reeled off were cartoonishly large. And she was talking about only one wedding. I have three daughters so I was mentally tripling everything. Tripling the cost, and tripling my anxiety.

I imagine those of you who have been through this whole wedding thing will laugh at my naïveté, but here's my problem: I am sentimental. I am sentimental far more than I am practical. I get misty eyed watching home-movies. I sometimes buy my daughters gifts that are out of our price range. In fact, and I'm not kidding here, I love my daughters so much that I would gladly give up a life-sustaining internal organ like a pancreas or a spleen if they needed it.

And when it comes to a wedding for one of my girls, I want to go all out. I'm talking about a big, fat, Protestant wedding. I'm imagining a wedding cake as big as a tool shed; truffles and champagne for three hundred; engraved Rolexes for all the guests; candelabras on every table; and maybe Dave Matthews playing for the reception before the bride and groom are whisked off in a private helicopter to Banff or Jost Van Dyke or some other equally exotic and hard to pronounce locale. You get the idea.

I love each of my daughters so much, I would gladly do this for them. But the problem I have -I know you've seen this coming- is that I don't have a big bag of money sitting around marked: "Enormously Large Bag of Cash to Pay for Three Lavish Weddings."

My budget for a wedding reception, if it were to happen right now, would be more along the lines of wild flowers stuck in a Mason jar perched on a picnic table in the back yard while guests help themselves to a bucket of KFC.

My solution…well….I really don't have a solution.

My two oldest are still in high school and the third daughter is in elementary school, so, presumably, this means I've got some more time to worry…and possibly save.

I would like to say, for the record, (and this is where I expect those of you who have done the big wedding thing before are really going to start laughing) that I would like to try to keep these future wedding expenses to a minimum. It's either that, or I could look into selling off my body parts. I wonder which I can get more money for…a pancreas or a spleen?

The Hungry Pioneer

———•••———

I completely blew my diet yesterday.

I blew it so badly, I may have to eat nothing but celery for a month before my calorie count falls into a normal range.

I know this is no excuse, but my car was being inspected and this all-you-can-eat place was right across the street. And this wasn't just any all-you-can-eat place; it was The Pioneer restaurant in Archdale.

And did I mention it was right across the street?

Diet or no diet, I'm just not good around that much temptation, particularly when there is a salad bar involved.

You see, I'm the type of guy who gets excited around large tubs of salad dressings.

Plus any restaurant that hangs a sign saying to use a clean plate each time you return and where Heinz 57, Worcestershire, Ketchup, A-1, vinegar and Texas Pete are permanent fixtures on table, is dear to my heart.

So, I said to myself what I imagine all dieters say when they decide to cheat, "Look Mac…. you've been doing good. Really good. You've lost eight pounds since July. You've been jogging and drinking those protein smoothies with ground flax seed for months now. One little trip to The Pioneer isn't going to hurt. Perhaps, you can just start with a salad."

But I knew deep down that if I was going to cheat, I was going to cheat big. I wasn't going to hold back. After all, we're talking about heaping ladles of Ranch dressing here.

So, with my initial guilt postponed, at least for a time, I allowed myself a broad grin as I heaped a glorious pile of iceberg lettuce onto my plate.

I shamelessly topped the mass of greenery with croutons, real Bac'os (not real bacon mind you, but real Bac'os Imitation Bacon Bits –which, at least in my mind, are far superior), cottage cheese, raisins, pickle spears, pickle slices, shredded ham, grated cheddar, half a boiled egg, black olives, those yummy little slices of pepperoni and a jalapeno pepper. But the best part, for me, is the dressing. (Buffet lines are an open invitation to pour three, four, or perhaps five different kinds of dressing onto one's salad. My motto is, "Ranch, Thousand Island, French and Vinaigrette– don't mind if I do.")

I estimated my, now brimming, plate weighed about four pounds as I hauled it back to the table.

On the next trip, I gave some thought to which foods on the buffet would be the best vehicle for each sauce on the table. Hmmmm…that prime rib will go nicely with that 57 sauce, I thought. And oooh, I bet those home fries will be good soaked in some ketchup. A little vinegar for that fried okra….Nice.

Like an honest to goodness pig, I gorged myself on all manner of delicious meats, vegetables and starches and topped each with a variety of sauces and gravies. I just couldn't help myself. It had been such a long time since I had eaten at a place like this. I had forgotten how absolutely wonderful all-you-can-eat buffets are.

I could already feel my waistline expanding as I selected a dish of Oreo pudding for dessert.

The delicious pudding, the meat, and the salad bar. The gravies and sauces. It was all simply wonderful.

Tomorrow, I'll need to start back with the protein smoothies and the jogging, I thought, because the only exercise I'm going to get today is waddling back across the street to get my car, and perhaps the effort of loosening my belt a bit.

While the Kids are Away

———•••———

Ok. I admit it. We hit rock bottom. My wife and I started dressing the cat.

I know. It sounds pretty stupid doesn't it?

Well, I have an explanation, sort of.

You see, for the first time in twenty-one years, all three of our kids were out of the house at the same time. Summer camp.

This left my wife and me home alone for two weeks.

So, you may be asking, what did you do with all this time on your hands? Well, we started out by doing all the predictable things you might expect an active couple who suddenly finds themselves without any children to care for might do. Night at the Movies: Check. Out for dinner: Check. Shopping at Friendly Center: Check. Completely cleaning-out two rooms in the house: Check.

Then, to our surprise, we realized we still had 12 more days of childlessness to go.

So what now?

"Have we hit rock bottom?" I asked.

My wife shrugged.

"Hey I know." I said over dinner, and only half joking. "Let's dress the cat in silly outfits and text the pictures to the girls while they're away."

My wife, Michele, looked at me for a moment, as if she was trying to work out what I had just said, then to my surprise she grinned and said, "Alright. But I think we'll need to dress her in the bathroom and close the door so she won't run away."

And that is how we began our first ever Extreme Feline Makeover.

Michele went to our daughter's room and began searching for all the clothes that we've accumulated over the years from Build-A-Bear Workshop, while I went searching for Severus, (Sev for short), our female grey tabby cat.

I found the cat outside lounging under my wife's car.

Please don't think that we were seriously dressing up the cat, as in, sitting back and doting admiringly at our work while thinking to ourselves: "oh how cute" or "oh how adorable."

No.

My wife and I were laughing our butts off as we tugged, pulled and fought a Welcome to Myrtle Beach teddy bear shirt over the head of our squirming and growling grey tabby.

Just as Michele wrestled and fought the shirt onto the cat. She yelled at me, "Quick. Take the picture! She's going to jump."

I did. I took the picture. In fact, I took lots of photos. Sev in a hoodie. Sev in a rainbow-colored baseball hat. Sev in a skirt and blouse.

What's more, all the shots turned out badly. Most were blurry because the cat kept trying to dart away as soon as Michele loosened her grip. But, some photos were bad in a good way, if you know what I mean.

My favorite is a shot taken while my wife had just finished muscling Sev into a chocolate brown t-shirt and is trying to position her paws into a pair of miniature soccer cleats. I like it because the cat seems to be wearing an expression of complete disgust. It's about as unnatural, contrived and hokey a pose as one can possibly imagine, and the cat seems to know this. But my favorite part is that you can clearly see my wife's arms in the background.

We texted the photograph of the cat in soccer cleats to our girls, with the caption: "I'm ready to play some soccer!"

Our oldest was the first to respond.

I think I was expecting her to join in the fun, but instead her reply read: "Is this all you have to do while we are gone?"

And the answer, sadly, is yes.

It was at this moment that I realized: you know you've really hit rock bottom when you start dressing your cat in teddy bear clothes.

Long Family Car Trip

———•••———

As far as long family car trips go, I'm a battle hardened veteran.

I've been pelted with every whiny, how-much-farther-tell-her-to-stop-she's-bothering-me-how-much-farther-is-it-I'm-bored-how-much-farther type of question from the back seat you can think of.

I've dealt with vomit and snowstorms. I've changed diapers and flat tires. I've handled fights, fusses, squabbles, and tiffs without even letting go of the steering wheel. I've even cleaned up after a box turtle, we picked up along the roadside, which promptly decided to pee on top of box of fresh croissants as soon as we got him inside the car.

My wife can tell you that I've threatened to pull over the car about 300 times and she can tell you about the one time I actually did.

But now, my daughters are mostly grown-up at ages 21, 18 and 13, and I've been at this family trip thing for a good long time.

So over the holidays, the girls and I drove to Florida. And I thought I was prepared for anything, but, as you may have guessed, I wasn't.

What I wasn't prepared for was: SILENCE.

Complete and total silence.

Each of my daughters was so entranced by whichever laptop, i-pad or i-phone device they happened to be staring into at the time…we'd go for long stretches where no one made any sound at all.

Our car was as loud as a rolling morgue, and about as lively.

In a strange way, I found myself longing for a small squabble to break out in the back seat. I wished that someone would ask how much farther, anything to break the silence.

What I got was total monotony.

Further and further into the trip, and in a strange reversal of roles, I discovered that I was the one who asked the questions from the front seat. "Anybody want to play that game where we try to see how many different state license plates we can count?"

In response, my youngest pulled the headphone away from her ear and asked, "Did you say something Dad?"

My oldest said, "Sure. I'll play," but in a tone of voice that lacked any excitement.

"Ok. Lets' play!" I said charging ahead anyway. "Who's going to keep a list of all the states we find?"

This question was met with more silence.

And so it went, for a long, long way.

I drove and drove while my daughters watched and watched.

At one point, I offered gamely, "There's one from Ohio," hoping to arouse some interest.

This was met with silence.

A few miles later I spotted another, "Michigan," I said.

More silence.

I found myself looking to see if I could spot a turtle along the roadside.

I suppressed a grin and thought: I'll bet a little turtle pee in the car would liven things up a bit.

I couldn't help but reflect –I had plenty of time for reflection after all– that when my kids were little, I would have loved just a little more peace and quiet. And now that my kids are older, I'm longing for a little more interaction.

A Case of Grease on the Brain

———•••———

HIGH POINT, NC – For seven torturous days, area resident, Mac Lane, has had the ridiculously catchy songs from the musical Grease echoing inside his head.

According to sources, ever since Lane watched the DVD featuring John Travolta and Olivia Newton John with his three daughters, he has been helplessly humming such nonsensical ditties as shoo-bop-shoo-wadda-wadda-yipitty-boom-de-boom and rama-lama-lama-ke-ding-a-de-dinga-a-dong for nearly all of his waking hours.

After seven days of relentless shoo-bop-shoo-bopping, Lane questions whether he can take it any more.

"It's like I've died, and gone to show tune hell," Lane said only moments after fighting back the urge to hum the phrase chang-chang-changity-chang-cha-chang for the nine-hundredth time.

The first indication that the 1950's style songs had completely penetrated his subconscious came the morning after, when the balding, father of three began a doing a half-hearted Hand Jive as he reached for his turning signal while driving his family to church. Shortly thereafter, Lane began unknowingly humming the chorus to Beauty School Dropout during the 8:45 worship service.

"Beauty School Dropout," Lane admitted. "I mean come on…."

Despite Lane's disgust with himself for humming such an embarrassing song, the smooth crooning of Frankie Avalon continued to haunt him throughout the rest of the day and into the night.

"It's not much fun trying to sleep when all you can think of are those maddeningly memorable songs from Grease. It's like John Travolta and Olivia Newton John are camping out in my skull."

The next morning Lane was confronted by a persistent urge to sing both the male and female parts of the film's climatic duet, "You're the One that I Want" while shaving.

On Wednesday, Lane allegedly did an abbreviated version of Travolta's Greased Lightin' dance in his office kitchenette when he thought no co-workers were looking. And on Thursday, he had difficulty keeping the phrase 'shoo-bop sha whada whadda yippidy boom da boom Chang chang changity chang shoo bop' from spilling out of his mouth during an important business meeting.

Lane has sung what portions of songs he can remember, like: Look at Me I'm Sandra Dee, Hopelessly Devoted to You, Summer Nights, Blue Moon, We'll Stay Together, and Greased Lightin' an estimated 10,784 times during the course of the week.

"Do you remember that girl on the news that couldn't get rid of her hiccups for more than a month?" a beleaguered Lane asked his wife, Michele. "I'm beginning to know how she felt."

"The only way to get rid of a song stuck in your head is to hear it again....In your case that would mean watching the whole movie....again," Michele said.

"There is no way I'm sitting through that movie again," Lane said. "I'd honestly rather have the hiccups, or a lobotomy, anything but this."

Dear University of South Carolina

———•••———

Dear University of South Carolina:

The reason I am writing you this letter is that my daughter is now living under your roof and not mine.

She's not upstairs, or in the shower, or in front of the computer. She's not leaving dirty clothes in great heaps on the floor or asking her mother what's for dinner.

I need you to know this because it's a big adjustment for our family. Except for the occasional sleep-over or summer camp, she has never lived anywhere else.

You first met her in the spring of her junior year in high school, when she and I visited on a campus tour. The azaleas and dogwoods were in full bloom, and the moment we stepped on campus, we felt welcome.

You were introduced that day to the beautiful, intelligent and confident young lady she has become, and not the little girl who, not very long ago, asked Santa Claus for a box of plastic snakes and lizards.

Among the acceptance letters she received, yours was, hands down, the best. (Whoever came up with the idea to send out acceptance packets in giant-sized envelopes with the Gamecock mascot emblazoned on it and mouthing the word "Yes!" is a genius and, in my opinion, should get an immediate raise.)

As an out-of-state student, the cost of attending your school was looking doubtful, until you offered her a whopper of an academic scholarship. For this we are hugely grateful.

Everyone was friendly and helpful on move-in day. Hauling in 78 pairs of shoes, curling irons, straightening irons, hair dryers, great quantities of bath gels, body washes along with mountains of clothes, designer bedding, and a refrigerator is never easy, but it went as smoothly as possible. Cocky, the mascot, even greeted my wife in the lobby of the dormitory.

Late that that evening, her mother, two younger sisters and I got back in the car. There were four of us in the car, but it felt empty without her with us. And, I admit it, I cried helplessly most of the way home. Her mother held up pretty well until she completely lost it in church the next morning. She cried so much that she left the building in the middle of worship and walked all the way home.

So now that my daughter is officially living on your campus, we expect you to challenge her. If you expect a lot from her, she will wildly exceed your expectations. That's the kind of person she is.

If for no other reason than it will make me feel better, I would like you know that she doesn't eat potatoes. I know. It's weird. But she's never liked them.

And I don't mean this in a bad way, but from your point of view, you have 4,550 incoming freshmen arriving this week. But from my perspective, you have my daughter arriving with 4,549 of her future classmates.

And if one thing outweighs all the rest, it would be our desire for you to keep her safe. She's more valuable to us than you can imagine, and I couldn't bear it if anything serious happened to her.

Also, if there is any way you can get her to eat potatoes, that would also be a big plus.

Note: The University of South Carolina contacted me after this column was published, asking if they could reprint it in their alumni news-letter. I readily agreed. USC featured this piece on the cover, and with a circulation of some 250,000, hundreds of emails followed from professors (each promising they would, in fact, challenge my daughter) and alumni. I even received a personal letter from USC President, Harris Pastides. Also, of note, my daughter, Carson graduated in 4 years (honors) with degrees in Economics and Spanish, and she is currently practicing law in Raleigh, NC. And, perhaps most remarkably, she's even started eating potatoes.

Back Yard Woes

———•••———

I think it's finally time to take down the old playset in the back yard.

Okay. Who am I kidding?

It was time to rip that sucker down three years ago.

It's been standing swing-less, canopy-less and –most importantly– child-less in my backyard for an embarrassingly long time.

Part of the problem is, there's no rule for this sort of thing. Nobody ever told me: after your youngest child blows out the candles at her twelfth birthday party, the very next thing you should do is demolish the swing set.

And none of my kids ever came inside after a long swing in the yard, poured a glass of lemonade from the fridge and said, "You know what dad? I'm done. You can go destroy the swing set now."

And because no one ever said anything, it's still there. Rotting.

Summer after summer, my youngest daughter, and kids from all over the neighborhood, were in our backyard happily swinging to and fro, giggling and singing -with a true joy that only kids of that age seem to possess- and then it stopped. But I'm not sure exactly when it stopped, only that it did.

Now, they are more interested in texting to and fro rather that swinging.

But the time has clearly come. My youngest daughter is as tall as her mom, and her sisters are in college. I suspected she had lost interest, but I wanted to ask just to make sure.

"Hey Anna. How would you feel if I took down the swing set this spring?" I ventured over breakfast.

I'm not sure what I was expecting, -maybe a little sadness. A tear or two. A touch of melancholy perhaps. I certainly wasn't expecting the reaction I got..... "Oh Dad. Pleeeease take it down. It looks terrible."

"It does look bad doesn't it?" I said eyeing the mildewing wood from the window.

I swallowed hard as I thought about the weekend my father-in-law, my dad and I poured the cement and sawed the lumber, shortly after we purchased the house. My oldest was three years old at the time, and she's 22 now.

We've had that swing set since before we had email, I thought.

I also thought about this absurd game that my daughters and I invented called "Tea and Tomato Juice" which involved the kids swinging back and forth pretending to throw either tea or tomato juice on my head while I pretended to be an attacking monster. It was an absurd game, and I must admit that I never understood exactly how it was played, but I am certain of how much we enjoyed ourselves on that swing set.

I also think about the countless times I pushed them as high as they could go. Or about the thousands of mosquitos I swatted from my legs as we passed the time on summer evenings. Or about how there once was a sandbox underneath the main structure until the cat discovered he could use it as his own private latrine. Or the times the girls tried to jump out as they were swinging to see how far they could fly.

I know. I know. I'm too sentimental about things like this. It's just a swing set after all.

But I just can't help being a little sad that once I take it down, I'll never be able to push my girls on it again.

Ever.

Driving with Anna

———•••———

I was working in the yard last weekend when my youngest child, Anna, came up to me and asked, "Hey Dad. Later today...maybe.... can we go have a driving lesson?"

I'm a little embarrassed to admit this, but my first thought was: if we go driving, then I'm not going to be able to get the grass mowed before dark. Plus, my wife was out of town and I had a great big list of things I wanted to get done before she got back.

And I'm sorry if this gets a little mushy, but maybe it was something about the freckles on her earnest young face, or perhaps it was the way she smiled at me with those teeth covered in braces. I don't know exactly what it was- but I can share with you that it was like an alarm bell went off inside my head. A wake-up call —as it were. I suddenly realized: the lawn can wait. In fact, all the chores I'd planned to do this weekend can wait. My daughter will never be this young again, and I need to seize this opportunity while I've still got it.

So, we went for a driving lesson and I loved every bouncy, jostling, herky-jerky minute of it —maybe more than she did.

About 15 minutes in, I thought: here I am. Here I am doing the most quintessential dad and daughter thing I can think of.... and I love this. I love how she sits bolt upright in the seat. I love how she checks her mirrors even though we were in the vacant parking lot of our church. I love how she gets out of the car to inspect her alignment into each parking space which in all candor– still needs a good bit of work. I love how we both laughed when she thought she was turning on the turn signal, only to discover that the windshield wipers had sprung to life and to her surprise the spray nozzles soaked the front glass with windshield cleaner.

How could I have even thought, even for an instant, about the lawn? Particularly in light of the fact that just this past fall, our second daughter has now flown the coop and left home for college.

With two gone, I've learned that once they go off to college, they really never come back. I mean yes, they do come back for holidays and summer break, but I've learned that they never really come back. In our case, the girls as they were when they left home, are gone. It's as if each has been replaced by a more confident, more independent and more self-sufficient version of their former selves. And I've also learned, my role in their lives is diminished.

Those stick-legged, pig-tailed girls that turned the music up way too loud and left their dirty laundry scattered all over the place are really gone.

I know. I know. My brain tells me that's exactly as it should be, and don't get me wrong, I wouldn't have it any other way. But my heart often wishes otherwise.

I have come to realize this: we really don't have much time left, Anna and I, and we need to make the most of it.

So, I hope you'll pardon me if I sign off now.

I think I'm going to ask Anna if she wants to go for another driving lesson.

Wet Cat Food Strains the Marriage

———•••———

I'm a huge dry-food guy.

If I had my way, our cats would subsist solely on those 50-pound bags of the cheapest, driest cat food I can find.

Here's a short list of the advantages of dry food.

1. It's dry.

2. It's dry.

3. It doesn't smell like the trash bin behind the fish market in July.

4. One doesn't need to use a spoon –a spoon which, by the way, will eventually be put into the dishwasher and will inevitably end up in my vanilla ice cream at some point later that day.

5. Did I mention, it's dry?

But of course, I don't have my way.

I know some couples who argue about finances; others quarrel about politics. I've even got a friend whose in-laws are a huge bone of contention in his marriage. I confess that my wife, Michele, and I have, at one time or another, fought over all the above, but here lately the biggest source of friction in our marriage has been cat food.

It's been a long, rolling argument that really just started in the past few months, when Michele started buying the wet stuff for the cats.

We've lived at the same address for 21 years, and in that time, we've had four cats.

Oliver, who happily ate dry food every day of his life, was completely healthy for 11 years, right up until the day my wife accidentally backed over him with the car.

Next, we had Fluffy. Fluffy was a dry food cat, right up until the day he mysteriously disappeared. We don't know exactly what happened to the Fluffster, but I'm pretty sure his diet wasn't to blame. Dave, our postman, thought it might be an owl.

Now, we have Tiger and Scooter. For years, both seemed completely content to eat the dry stuff as well, up until recently. The problem is that Tiger is getting old, and Michele has started coddling him. She thinks it's hard for him to chew in his old age, and the vet saw something in his throat that might be cancer, so, in response, Michele started buying both cats the wet canned stuff.

I was open-minded until I cracked the first can. I scarcely know how to describe how utterly vile and disgusting this stuff is. This stuff is so nasty, while I was opening a can of it this morning, a tiny speck dripped on my finger. I washed my hands immediately. Washed again when I got to work. A third time just now, and my finger still smells like a rotting mackerel head.

Another thing that bothers me is the names they use to describe what's inside the can. From the description, one would think you were at the finest restaurant in town: Cod, Sole and Shrimp. Natural Wild-Caught Alaskan Salmon. And White Chicken Entree' in a Delicate Broth.

I'm not kidding. And I didn't make this up.

If the cat food companies had any honesty at all the flavor descriptions should read: "Salmon Eyeballs with Factory Sweepings," or "Guts and Tripe in a Hearty Offal Gravy," or "Man. This Stuff Is Just Plain Nasty –with Real Liquefied Shrimp Sauce."

But with this said, I honestly don't know what the solution to my problem is.

Even with the cancer thing in Tiger's throat, and as old as he is, my bet is that he will live at least another three years.

I guess I can either keep fighting Michele or buy a clothespin for my nose and a pair of rubber gloves.

Poop Scoop Inc.

———•••———

"Uhhh Dad....what's that kid doing walking around in our back yard?" my oldest daughter asked.

"That kid, my dear, is not just any kid. That kid happens to be a very enterprising young man," I said.

"What's he doing back there?"

"He is picking up dog poop."

I could tell she was a bit puzzled, so I elaborated as I pointed out the window, using an expansive tone of voice, I said, "Since you've been away at college, you may not be aware of some of the changes we've made around the house. You see, since you've been gone we've hired Tanner Harron to pick up the dog doo from our yard. He's in the fifth grade and he's started his own business this summer called Poop Scoop."

We both watched him work for a few minutes.

"What I like is that he doesn't wander all over the yard....watch him... notice how he starts in the corner and walks back and forth in a regular pattern to make sure he doesn't miss anything. He really does a great job! But the best part is that at the end of each month, he sends us an invoice. It's a real invoice, itemized with each time he serviced our yard. It's awesome! I know he's only a fifth grader, but he's running this thing like a real business."

"And a few weeks ago," I continued with a how-great-is-that smile on my face.

"He found a dead chipmunk in the front yard. Apparently one of the cats killed it,

anyway, he scooped up the dead chipmunk at no extra charge."

"So how much does he charge?" she asked.

"I think a dollar."

I expected my daughter to be as excited as I was. Instead she looked horrified, "Is that all you pay him?"

"Well no….now that I think about it…maybe it's a dollar for the front and a dollar for the back. So, two dollars a week is what I think he charges. But I'm not sure. Let's ask him," I said opening the back door. "Hey, Tanner…. How much do you charge?"

With his yellow bucket in one hand and his spring-loaded-pooper-scooping-grapping-tool in the other, Tanner looked up from his work, "I charge a dollar for the front and a dollar for the back each time."

"And how many customers do you have Tanner?"

"I do the Painter's yard on Thursday, the Fishers' on Friday, the Henley's yard on Saturday and your yard on Sundays, and I've just added the Bells."

"You say you do the Henley's yard?" A.B. Henley is a city councilman in High Point and I couldn't resist prying a little bit. "Do the Henley's have a lot of poop?" I asked.

"Yeah," Tanner said with a smile. "They do have a lot of poop."

I'm not sure why, but it pleased me to know that Councilman Henley has a lot of poop in his yard.

Satisfied, I closed the door and did the math aloud, hoping to demonstrate to my college student daughter that I wasn't taking advantage of Tanner, but rather this 5th grader really had a nice business going.

"So Tanner has four houses that he services at $2.00 per week," I said. "That works out to $32.00 per month or $384.00 a year and that's before he adds the Bells….Not bad money for a fifth grader."

"Dead chipmunks Dad? I still don't think you are paying him enough."

"Well," I conceded. "I probably should have given him a little extra for picking up the dead chipmunk."

Fake Neighbors

——•••——

On my way home from work a few months back, I noticed a U-Haul truck in our neighbor's driveway. The house has been for sale and sitting empty about a year now, and I was happy to see some activity over there. I also wanted to meet the new folks, so I walked over, hand outstretched, to say hello.

In the driveway stood a middle-aged couple. "Are you the new neighbors?" I asked.

"No. Actually we are professional home-stagers," he said handing me a business card. "But, it's all been arranged. You'll be getting new temporary neighbors on Sunday."

Seeing my befuddled expression, the stager added, "They are a nice couple, both retired, and they'll only be living here as long as it takes to sell the house."

I've heard of house-staging before, but I thought it was just about decorating with sofas and pictures and stuff, I had no idea that things have advanced to the level of using actual people as props.

About an hour later, I told my wife, Michele, about my encounter.

"So, we're getting new neighbors," I explained. "But they are not like real neighbors. They don't plan to be there long-term…..only till the house sells."

Michele nodded.

"So, it's like we are getting fake neighbors," I added.

Michele laughed. "We've never had fake neighbors before."

"I know." I said. "What do we do? Should we take them a fake pie? You know, so as to give them a proper fake welcome."

"Do they have a fake dog and fake kids?"

We both laughed at that.

Which brings up the question: how does one treat a neighbor whom you know will only be there temporarily? One who may be pulling up stakes at any moment? We live on a sleepy little street with almost no traffic and very little turn-over. We still think of the family who moved in about 10 years ago, as the new guys on the block.

But the fake neighbors didn't turn out to be fake at all. This point was driven home by the fact that one afternoon, only a day or so after they moved in, Michele saw the husband, a balding, gray-haired man, strolling leisurely about in his new home wearing nothing but his skivvies. I guess maybe they hadn't had time to hang the fake draperies.

So, after having a few more good laughs about fake dogs and fake draperies, we decided to treat the fake neighbors like real neighbors. We brought them a real chicken pie, and gave them a real welcome. They introduced themselves as Raymond and Barbara, and shared that they were both retired and needed temporary housing after selling their home and while they shopped for another.

And for a couple of human props, they turned out to be interesting and like-able folks.

But now I'm told the house has sold for real this time. I guess the professional home-staging thing must have worked.

And once again, I'm planning to walk over with my hand out-stretched and say hello, only this time I might ask if I can help hang the draperies.

Owl Watching

———•••———

"This is amazing!" I said. "I think it's been the most exciting night of owl watching we've had yet."

We watched as the parent owl glided gracefully through the tree tops while the two younger juvenile owls followed, flying clumsily and bumping into small branches as they went.

"That was so cool," I said. "That could have been the baby owls' first flight."

"I don't know how many people I'd share that with," my wife, Michele, said.

"Getting excited about seeing owls....I don't know....it sounds so...."

"Nerdy?" I cut in with a smile still excited about the owls. "I've always embraced my inner nerd."

"No, not nerdy. That's not what I mean. It makes us sound more like....well... old-ish," she said.

"But we're not old," I said. "And we are definitely not 'ish'."

"We may be getting a bit on the 'ish' side," she said. "And I don't want you going around telling everybody that we are watching owls either. Watching birds is something old people do. Retired people who don't have young kids screaming and running around. People younger than us don't have time to go on walks in the evening and look at owls."

I didn't have a good come back for that one. Our oldest is 19 and our youngest is 11.

The owl thing began several weeks ago, when, on an evening walk through the neighborhood my wife and I watched open-mouthed as this giant-sized, blurr-of- a-bird swooped down in front of us and grabbed a chipmunk or a mouse or some other small critter off the ground. It was like seeing something out of Marlin Perkin's Wild Kingdom. Struck by how big he was up close, and what a formidable hunter he was, we took an interest and have looked for him on subsequent walks.

The next night we saw him (or it could be a female I guess) perched in a tree close to the same spot. Each night, for the next several nights we saw him again and again.

We've taken our three daughters down to see him. They named him Hedwig.

Thanks to the owl, I've changed my routine. Normally, I run in one direction while my wife walks in another, but since we began owl watching, I started jogging first then walking later with my wife, just to see the owl.

I came home from work the other night to find my wife camped out in front of the computer. As I entered the room, I heard hooting "WHOOO WHOOO" sounds coming from the computer speakers.

"What have you got going on here?" I asked.

"I'm listening to recorded owl calls," she said. "I'm trying to figure out what kind he is."

We spent about thirty minutes looking and listening to owls on-line. We decided Hedwig was a Barred Owl.

The next night, we heard a ruckus up in the tree tops. We saw not one, not two, but three Barred Owls clustered together in a tree. Further in the top of the tree, we noticed the nest.

I can't say for sure if it was baby owls' first flight, but the younger, smaller owls didn't look like they had the hang of flying yet. They both bumped along whacking into small branches as they went, my wife and I stood on the ground fascinated.

And, as you can see from the above conversation, my wife really wants to keep this owl watching thing a secret. So, I need your help.

Please don't tell anyone OK?

Ma's Caring

———•••———

I hope my grandmother is okay with me sharing this. She can be a private person and this story is personal.

But it's also a story that has touched me deeply: I've never heard my grandmother complain about caring for my grandfather.

Not once.

*Four and a half years ago a nasty stroke paralyzed the left side of my grandfa-*ther's body, robbing him of his mobility and much of his vitality.

Since that day since, my grandmother whom I call Ma, arrives by his bedside every morning at breakfast, and doesn't leave his side until after she's tucked him into bed that night.

The caregivers at The Village at Brookwood, an assisted living facility, marvel at my grandmother's devotion. They say they've never seen anyone quite like her. "She's an amazing woman" and "I don't know if I've ever seen a more devoted and loving wife," I've heard them say.

My mother comes two days a week and stays from 8:00 until 2:30, so my grandmother can go to the store and run errands, but barring that, Ma has been by his side all day, every day.

She's carried on this routine, selflessly, for four and half years. And what's even more remarkable is that I don't think she's ever missed a day. She's been there to spoon food into his mouth, and speak softly to him.

She calls him "Sweety."

She washes his clothes, shaves his face, and checks behind the caregivers to make certain everything is done to her high standards. She also has an uncanny ability to anticipate his needs.

And what's even more remarkable, is that I've never heard her even imply that she considers this a chore. I bellyache about taking out the garbage, yet my grandmother has sat by his bedside either feeding him, talking to him or quietly playing solitaire in his room for months and months.

If you ask her, and I have, she'll say, "I took those sickness and health wedding vows seriously."

On Tuesday, my grandfather stopped eating. On Wednesday, the doctor gave us the "could go at anytime" speech with the family gathered around his bedside.

Ma and I were walking down the hallway and I told her that she has taught me and my children a lot about how to grow old and about how to care for someone you love. I told her that my three daughters have seen her love and devotion and that they will remember it always. She responded by saying, "I'm just doing what I want to do." As if it's no big deal. And to me that's what makes her devotion so much more special. She's not doing it to get points from anyone, she is simply doing it because she wants to.

As I'm writing this, my grandfather is slipping away. He is struggling to breath and the nurses are giving him morphine every two hours or so.

My heart is breaking and I know this must be even harder for my grandmother.

I've broken down in tears several times, but my grandmother has remained rock-steady. My grandmother sits beside him gently putting balm on his lips. She kisses his forehead and whispers "I love you Sweety" into his ear.

We all know the end is near. We've been praying, crying, and sometimes laughing around his bedside.

His great-grandchildren have been there. My aunt and uncle; my mother and stepfather; and my wife and I have surrounded him with love in these last days.

On Saturday night, when the end looked very close, she stayed up all night refusing to leave his bedside.

The following afternoon, around 2:00, my grandfather breathed his last breath.

My grandmother was right there by his side. She held his hand as he went to be with God, and I can't help but think: that's the way it should be.

She was caring for him right up until the very last......until death do us part.

Camp Win-Win Situation –Offers an Alternative to Traditional Summer Camps

———•••———

Corporate language camps are becoming an increasingly popular option for parents seeking to give their child an early leg-up into the business world.

"Our camp is essentially a language camp for kids to learn the terminology and jargon of business," said Arthur Zelnik, Assistant Director for Camp Win-Win Situation located in Raleigh, NC.

"By summer's end, campers as young as 5 years-old are confidently bandying about such phrases as 'paradigm shift' and 'seamless integration' with the zest and energy of a seasoned corporate middle-manager," said Zelnik.

Local parent, Daniel Smithson, was hesitant at first. "My son had some doubts about going to a business camp. For a while, he considered a sailing camp on the coast, but as soon as he got to Camp Win-Win, he loved it. His favorite activity is playing phone tag."

Smithson added, "I really think it's preparing him for life ahead. I mean let's be honest…how often does one need to weave a lanyard keychain or shoot a bow and arrow or paddle a canoe in the real world?"

In addition to Phone Tag, some of the activities offered by Camp Win-Win include: Giving 110%; Touching Base; Moving the Cheese; Pushing the Envelope; Dropping the Ball; Thinking Outside the Box, and Staying in the Loop.

Jimmy Nichols, age 8, and three-year veteran of the camp, offered the following testimonial: "The camp is really neat. It's the go-to camp. At the end of the day, it's the best camp in terms of being a client-centered value."

"The youngest campers start out with more basic corporate jargon," said Rachel Shelly, a business major at a local college, and third session counselor. "They begin with simple phrases like 'user-focused' and 'best-practices,' while the older campers master the pronunciation of such terms as 'seeking integrated solutions' and 'core competency.'

The scenic, 83 acre property, where the original Camp Sunshine thrived for 47 years, was sold to a real estate development firm in October, 2006. Camp Win-Win Situation's new location is on the 3rd floor of The Plaza Parke Building, 10047 Airport Rd. Suite # 373-B. The fax machine, filing cabinets, the computer system and one leather swivel chair are the only surviving artifacts from the old camp.

According to Camp Win-Win Situation's Summer Programs Executive Administrator, Michael Huggins, "I think we're really on to something here. Since we made the change from Camp Sunshine to Camp Win-Win Situation, our enrollment is through the roof."

"Plus our overhead is like a thousand times less since we sold off the canoes, the horses, and all that wooded land." Huggins said. "This has been a hugely profitable move for us....and the kids seem to like camping in an office setting. There's no manure smell, no snakes, no poison ivy, no sun burn. It really is a win-win for everyone."

The camp plans to expand its activities this summer to include Casual Friday, where each Friday, the young campers need not dress in coat and tie.

Plastic, but Perfect

———•••———

Yesterday, I drove past a furniture showroom near downtown High Point. Out front, was what appeared to be a perfectly manicured lawn. What was so startling, is that just a few days ago, this space was a parking lot. Pavement. And now, suddenly….poof….here is this lush green grass.

I circled the block to have another look, and as you've probably guessed, it wasn't actually grass. It was some sort of artificial grass-like substitute, but man did it look good. I stopped the car, got out, and took a few steps. It was perfect. Plastic, but perfect.

For the rest of the day, I could scarcely think of anything else. You see, I think a lot about grass this time of year, because, my lawn and I have been waging war for some two decades now.

It always starts the same. Each spring, I set out. Filled with hope, I seed. I water. I fertilize, aerate, and put down the expensive stuff that is positively guaranteed to prevent crabgrass.

The years have taught me that no one ever really gets rid of crabgrass, the best you can hope for is to stave it off for a while. To this point, years ago, I heard a man say the only fool-proof way to get rid of crabgrass is to move, and I believe him.

So it is, that each springtime, I cling to the hope things will turn out differently, but in my heart, I know that by late July, once again I'll be looking out over a brown, scorched, weed-filled plot of earth with bare spots the size of ping pong tables.

You know the guy in mythology that pushes a giant stone uphill for all eternity, but never quite gets to the top? That's the way it is with my lawn. Just when I think I've gotten it looking pretty good, The Fates conspire to thwart me. It's as if they are having a conversation…..'Say, Mac down there has almost gotten those bare patches filled in….His grass looks way too green and leafy. Should we send a drought or a colony of moles? Both! Good thinking! And let's make sure that nest of squirrels stays healthy so they can dig another 10,000 tiny holes in the front part where all the neighbors can see it."

Kidding aside, in addition to the squirrels and their relentless digging, I had moles for the first time ever this spring. My entire front yard felt like I was walking on a bed of giant-sized sponge cake.

Moles! Honestly. Moles?

It's gotten to the point where something's got to give. And this is why I've been thinking so much about this plastic turf stuff. I honestly don't know if I have got the guts, or the budget to go all in and carpet my whole yard with the stuff, but I must confess that I'm really, really tempted.

I can imagine the look on my neighbor's face as I roll out this grassy green perfection, pausing occasionally, shout up at the tree top squirrels. "Try and dig up this up you destructive little vermin!" Or making rude and emphatic hand gestures at the ground, "Go ahead Mr. Mole. Dig under this stuff all you want. It's plastic Buddy."

Do you see how nuts this whole yard thing makes me? Do you see? I'm a grown man, and father of three, and I'm actually imagining myself yelling and gesturing profanely at small rodents!

And the worst part is: even if I did cover my yard in this turf stuff, I imagine the crabgrass will still find a way to choke out and kill even plastic."

The Fish and the Guide

———•••———

I need to make a full confession.

Yes. I caught a monster fish –a 28" brown trout. And yes, as you can probably already tell, I have been bragging shamelessly – to basically anyone who'll listen.

And thanks to social media, namely Facebook, I've made sure everyone from my mother to my 9th grade history teacher has seen the photo of me clad in hip waders holding this water buffalo with fins.

So, based on this, one might think I'm a great…or skilled….or knowledgeable… or at least a competent trout fisherman, but I'm not.

I'm really not.

It started like this: my father and I were invited to go on this trout fishing expedition hosted by John Weir, who had lined up a group of us to fish the waters of north Georgia for long a weekend.

On the first day, we were introduced to our guides. Dad and I would be fishing with a stern and crusty guide named John Rice. Think Sargent Carter with dry flies hooked to his vest. John told us that he'd been a guide in this area for 8 years and last year according to his taxes, he guided 127 days in 2015.

Naturally, on my first cast with John, I got my line hung in a tree. A rhododendron to be exact, and from there, I proceeded to make a total mess of everything. I hung my fly in seemingly every hemlock tree, pine tree, and rhododendron bush on either bank and sometimes overhead. I became quite good at creating large bird-nest size tangles that I had to ask John to come help me fix.

It was humiliating.

I joked about it the first few times I got hung up, but it soon ceased being funny.

"Uh, John. I'm sorry, but I've gotten hung......again."

To which John replied, "How'd you do that? I told you to roll cast. You can't get hung if you are only roll casting."

My neck reddened with shame as he cut my line and retied my rig over and over. Each time, I tried to follow John's instructions, and each time I seemed to screw it up somehow. There were times I felt like a third grader who'd been scolded for misbehaving.

As the day progressed, I tried to only cast where John said to cast and to stand exactly where he said to stand, and thanks to John's tutelage, I started catching fish, culminating in my 28" trophy trout.

This whole story reminded me of how much of my life has been a lot like this trout fishing trip. And how many times a good guide (or coach or mentor) has come to the rescue.

So, my confession is this: while I got all the glory for landing the monster trout, it was really John Rice who rightfully should get all the credit not me....unless there is a prize for the most tangled-up line.

Pa$$w8rd Nightm@re!

────●●●────

In order to turn on my computer, the tech guy at work said I'd need to remember the following new password: MAC^+{LAnE$SAles$#+@!!)): or something equally as befuddling and complex.

I called him up and said, "Look Jim. There is no way I'll ever remember this. Not in a million years."

"OK, What can you remember?"

"How about….m…a…c?"

"That's not strong enough."

"What if we capitalize the M?" I offered hopefully.

"Nope," he said -deadpan. "It needs to have punctuation, letters in upper and lower case, 3 Chinese characters, and a note from your doctor in order to be effective." (That wasn't exactly what he said, but you get the gist.)

"This new password is longer than the alphabet," I pleaded.

"It's only 19 characters," Jim said.

"Come on. It's not like we are sitting on nuclear missile secrets here. We sell upholstery fabric for crying out loud! Who would ever want to hack us? Fabric Junkies? Or some crazed interior designer looking for decorative damasks?"

After twenty minutes of intense negotiations, Jim agreed to drop a colon. A colon!

And even without the colon, my password still seemed more elaborate than the German Enigma Code.

What brought this story about Jim and the dropped colon to mind, is that I read an article yesterday about the man who actually wrote THE book on password management. Apparently, back in 2003, a man named Bill Burr, who worked for the National Institute of Standards and Technology, wrote an 8 page guide advising how to protect accounts by using increasingly complex passwords that included all those impossible to remember symbols and punctuation. Banks, colleges, the government —and every business you can think of— adopted his guidelines with gusto…..and…in so doing, made all our lives just that much more frustrating.

But guess what? The article went on to say that Bill Burr recently made a confession:

> He admitted he blew it. That's right. All those ^*#$?><!! are not only unnecessary, but, there is now proof that all those preposterously hard to remember passwords -meaning those that are filled with symbols and punctuation- are easier to hack than just a simple combination of words. So, ihatepasswords is apparently harder to crack than I_H@tepa$$wRds.

As soon as I'm done writing this, I think I'll call our tech guy Jim and ask if he read the article on Bill Burr's confession. Maybe I can get him to change my password to: cannotrecall

That's a password I don't think I'll have a problem remembering.

Threadbare

———•••———

I was leafing through one of those ultra-high-end, ultra-high fashion design magazines the other day, when I spotted a photograph that stopped me cold.

The image featured was in a pictorial of a house that had been decorated by some fancy Frenchman —with five names and four hyphens and a Yves thrown in for good measure. Anyway, right in the middle of one of the interior shots, were a pair of chairs that looked like a cat…no…no…not a cat, something bigger than a cat…it looked like a full-grown Bengal tiger, had shredded the fabric to tatters.

I couldn't believe my eyes.

I became so excited that I tore the page out of the magazine and image of the ragged chair home to show my entire family.

"Look at this! Look at this!" I said waving the magazine photo around crazily in the air.

My three daughters and my wife gathered around to see what all the fuss was about.

"I have, in my hand, a magazine from my office," I announced. "As you know, we live in the Furniture Capital of the World. Trends are set here. Styles for the home begin here in High Point. And you all know, the designers where I work subscribe to all the latest home fashion magazines. They want to be right on top of every trend in furnishing from around the world. This particular magazine that I'm about to show you is so fancy it makes Architectural Digest look like backwoodsy. It makes Elle Décor look like Jed and Granny Clampett."

"Featured in this magazine are two chairs…" I paused for dramatic effect…"that look like a tiger used them for a chew toy." Gesturing to the photograph I said,

"Can you all see that? Can you all see the upholstery fabric has been shredded to ribbons on these chairs?"

I got nods all around.

"Do you know what this means?" and as I asked this question, I pulled one of our own upholstered chairs from under the dining room table so everyone could see.

"Do you see how the fabric has split completely open on this chair in our house? Can you see the stuffing is bulging out crazily? Can you see how the material is completely disintegrated? This French designer with all the hyphens in his name apparently knows that you don't rush out and recover a chair just because the fabric has become a tad threadbare. In fact, it says here that he created these chairs to look distressed."

"This magazine has let me know we need not be ashamed to invite guests into our home over the holidays just because our chairs are a mess. I feel so strongly about this, that I am stating for the record, right now, that our dining chairs are no longer an eyesore. I am hereby declaring these to be a fashion statement!"

The kids were game, but my wife, Michele, wasn't buying it.

"Right here in our dining room, we are on the fore-front of the world fashion," I continued gesturing to the exposed padding and stuffing. "We are taking shabby chic to a whole new level."

Of course, my wife knows I wasn't really serious. She knows that I was just trying to make light of the fact that we are trying to put-off spending the money to recover the chairs for a time. With one child in college and another close behind, my wife Michele and I had agreed to just live with the threadbare chairs for a while, to save a few bucks.

When the kids left the room, my wife whispered to me, "Leather. I think we need to recover them in leather....but not until after Christmas."

"I agree," I admitted. "But they won't be as fashionable."

It's All About the Gear

—•••—

I accepted an invitation to hike a 26 mile segment of the Appalachian Trail recently with three friends, but almost immediately, I began to have some misgivings.

We met to organize the hike and immediately afterward, I admitted to my wife, Michele, "I think I'm in way over my head. These guys are serious hikers."

"You're in good shape. You jog all the time. What are you worried about?"

"It's the gear," I said. "I knew I was in trouble when Dan started with: I can't wait for you guys to see my new Inflatable Klymit Inertia X Frame Ultralight Sleeping Pad. It weighs 9.7 ounces and it folds up smaller than a pack of cigarettes. Apparently he told Martha (his wife) that he wouldn't be coming to bed for the next few nights, because he'd be testing it out on the floor of his office to see how it goes."

"And then John said, 'Two hikes ago, I brought a pair of Keen sandals, in addition to my hiking boots. And can you believe they weighed 26 ounces?' ….as John was saying this the two other guys, Ray and Dan, were looking at him with an expression that seemed to say what a fool John must be to have even considered packing such preposterously heavy footwear as a pair of 26 ounce sandals. Their demeanor suggested he may as well have been carrying a cannonball in his backpack. But, John went on to say that last spring he packed his Vibram Five fingers. He said they weighed 17 ounces. But he still thought that was too much, so he took his scale to Walmart and weighed various shoes in the store before settling on a pair of slip-ons that only weigh 11 ounces."

"Are you hearing this?" I said to Michele. "The man took a set of scales to Walmart to weigh shoes! And the net result is that he saved six ounces. That's like half a ham sandwich worth of weight. I learned theses guys weigh everything….down to the ounce. They talk about the weight endlessly."

"So, what did you do?" Michele asked.

"Mostly I just tried to frown and look grim whenever anything sounded too heavy, but I think I got it wrong once or twice. Dan told me his sleeping bag weighed 21.5 ounces, so I frowned. But apparently that's really good for a sleeping bag and he paid a small fortune to buy one that only weighed so little because it's filled entirely with some sort of scientific material that weighs less than a single helium atom or some such thing."

"The longer I sat there the more I realized that I was hopelessly out of my league. And the worst thing is they have a weigh-in. If your pack is over 30 pounds on the day of the hike, they threatened to remove items. My heart sank as I imagined Ray with his arms folded like an airport security guard, confiscating my dry socks, clean underwear and travel size toothpaste due to an overweight pack."

So, fast forward three weeks. We completed the hike, and because of their meticulous preparation, none of us had any trouble of any kind. In fact, quite the opposite, it was a total pleasure.

And I admit, after slogging up and down mountains for 26 miles, with a 30 pound on my back, I understand a little better why these guys are so obsessed with the weight thing.

My only problem is whether I should tell these guys that I still think sleeping on the office floor and carrying a scale to Walmart to weigh shoes is a little much.

I think maybe I'll keep that to myself….after all….I had a great time, and I want to get invited back.

Thin Mints Are
Apparently Universal

———•••———

"Dad! I've made a discovery," my daughter said over the phone....she's away at college in Virginia and I could hear the excitement in her voice. "Girl Scout Cookies aren't the same everywhere!"

"What do you mean they're not the same?" I asked.

"This afternoon some Girl Scouts had a table set up in front of the Student Union. I bought 2 boxes of Thin Mints, a box of Caramel Delights, and a box of Peanut Butter Patties. I bought them so I could share with the girls in my suite. I mean who doesn't like Girl Scout Cookies right? Only, when I got back to the dorm, I showed my cookies to Catherine and Kristina and they were horrified."

"What?" I said "Why on earth would they be horrified by Girl Scout Cookies?"

My daughter said, "Well.....Kristina is from Atlanta and Catherine is from Tennessee, and neither had ever heard of Caramel Delights or Peanut Butter Patties before."

"Really?"

"Yeah. Really. They acted like my cookies were some sort of cheap counterfeit knock-offs."

"That's crazy business," I said.

"Yeah. I know. Both of them said that where they come from Peanut Butter Patties aren't called Peanut Butter Patties at all. Apparently they call them Tagalongs.

And Caramel Delights are named Samoas."

"Who's ever heard of a Samoa or a Tag-a-Long?" I said.

"Here's where it gets weird. I've asked around....girls from California, New York, and Virginia some grew up with Tagalongs some with Peanut Butter Patties. It's about 50-50. One of the girls said my cookies were just wrong and accused me of trying to corrupt her childhood. People can get really defensive about cookie names."

"What about Thin Mints?" I asked. "Do they have another name for those too?"

"Apparently everybody calls them Thin Mints. Thin Mints are universal."

So to get to the bottom of the Tagalong vs. Peanut Butter Pattie dispute, I decided to phone our local supplier of Girl Scout Cookies: nine year old Arden Yates of Girl Scout Troop 2114 who lives in our neighborhood and who, incidentally, sold my wife four boxes of cookies last week.

"Hi Arden," I said. "Can I ask you a couple of questions?"

"Sure Mr. Lane."

"I understand you are selling Girl Scout Cookies."

"Yes sir," she said.

I was immediately impressed by how incredibly polite and articulate she was on the telephone, "How many boxes have you sold?"

"I've sold a lot."

"How many is a lot?"

"About 250 boxes."

"Whoa! That is impressive. How did you manage to sell so many?" I asked.

"I went to my Grandmother's house and we went to see all of her friends in her neighborhood. She has a lot of friends."

"Did anybody tell you no?"

"No sir."

As adorable and well-spoken as Arden Yates is, I think one would have to possess super-human powers of resistance to tell her no. As I mentioned, our family bought four boxes and if I wasn't on this gluten free diet, I know my wife would have easily bought double that.

"OK," I said, getting down to business. "Have you ever heard of a cookie called a Tagalong or a Samoa?"

"No sir." she said.

"Thank you Arden. And congratulations on selling so many cookies."

According to the official website, the Girl Scouts use different bakers so the cookie names can vary depending on which baker supplies which troop.

Here is the complete list of all the cookies that have different names in different regions:

> Caramel Delights = Samoas
> Peanut Butter Patties = Tagalongs
> Do-si-dos = Peanut Butter Sandwich
> Short Bread = Trefoils
> And of course, Thin Mints are universal.

Isn't it amazing what you can learn in college?

Have You Tried Shaving with Your Readers On?

————•••————

In the wild, the male octopus is such a devoted father that he completely stops taking care of himself in order to devote all his time, energy and strength to raising his young. In fact, he ignores his own well-being so much, that as soon as his offspring reach a certain age, the male octopus, is so spent, that he dies.

I know this is going to sound weird, but I was thinking about this when I attended a charity thing the other evening. A good friend of mine came over to shake hands. As we spoke, I noticed he had missed a spot, about the size of a nickel, on the side of his face when he was shaving. It was like he was trying to grow a misplaced soul-patch.

Now if this guy was in his eighties or nineties I could understand, but this guy was in his mid-fifties. As we talked, all I could think of was: have you tried wearing your readers when you shave?

At the same event, I noticed how many of my contemporaries had started slipping in the area of personal appearance. Dated neckties, nose hair, and outdated suits. And let me say first that I get it. Much like the male octopus, most men I know, who are in their 50's and 60's have put themselves on the back-burner. The very back burner. Am I right guys? You would much rather buy your daughter a $500 prom dress, or put $500 dollars down on a freshman meal plan, than purchase a new sport coat for your self right? Not to mention, if you are like me, you're already drowning in college tuition, data plans, health insurance, car insurance, on and on.

It's as if dads like us have thought about everyone else for so long that it's become ingrained. Habitual. You've made yourself such a low priority that you don't shave as carefully as you once did, nor, care as much about your wardrobe.

Maybe you still got a few printed Jerry Garcia ties from the 1990's hanging in your closet?

Maybe your pants are of the wide-leg and cuffed-bottom variety?

If so, I want you to know this: there are lots of other octopus dad's out there just like us, and we don't have to roll over and die just yet. We can still rock a cocktail party, or a business function.

So, I've done a little homework and put together a short list of suggestions:

> If you can't clearly see your face, put your readers on when you shave. Seriously. You need to get a good look at what you are doing so you can shave properly.

> Long hairs protruding from the end of your nose, ears, nostrils, and eyebrows is not a good look. Seriously guys. Look at yourself, either with the reading glasses or in one of those up-close mirrors like my wife has that magnifies everything like 25 times, and start plucking.

> Chuck all neckties acquired before 2015. Yes. Even that Father's Day gift from whatever year the kids gave it to you....especially printed and novelty ties. These are so far gone and out of style Goodwill doesn't want them anymore. And while you're at it; occasions where neckties are mandatory are becoming less and less frequent, so instead of having 10-20 ties in your closest that are just passable, why not have 1 or 2 that are simply killer? My suggestion is to spend a few bucks and buy 1 or 2 really, really nice ties and ditch the rest.

> Suits and sport coats: each time we get a new president, you should buy a new suit or sport coat. If you've got an Obama, a Bush or even a Clinton hanging in your closet, it's time for an update.

> Same goes for pants: wide leg trousers with cuffs date you worse than you know.

We may still be octopus dads, but at least we'll be well-dressed and well-groomed octopus dads.

Trouble Avoided at Parent's Weekend

————•••————

The trouble started about an hour and a half into the drive.

My wife, Michele, and I left the house early that Saturday morning -with our youngest, Anna, in the backseat- to go see our middle daughter, Cannon, at Parent's Weekend in Charlottesville, Virginia.

I sprung for a nice hotel room. Her sorority was hosting a formal for all the parents....sit-down dinner...band...the works.

As I steered the car through the winding mountain roads, Anna piped up from the back seat, "Uh Dad....can you not say anything embarrassing this weekend?

Cannon isn't going to like it if you embarrass her in front of her college friends."

"What?" I asked, a bit taken aback. "Me? Embarrassing? What do I say that's embarrassing?"

"Potty-talk," Anna said.

"I agree," My wife added. "You talk about bathroom stuff a lot."

"It's disgusting when you do that," Anna added.

"Is that it? Is there anything else I do that's horribly offensive?"

And without missing a beat Anna said, "You always mention how expensive everything is." My wife nodded in hearty agreement, "That really makes Cannon mad."

"So what is this? Are you guys making some kind of list?"

"Good idea. I think we should make you a list," Michele said.

Anna took an index card from her school backpack and began writing. At 14, I could tell she was thrilled the prospect of writing down a list of rules for dad. She began, "I'm going to make of list of all the things you are not allowed to say this weekend: 1. No mention of any bodily functions. 2. No bringing up old boyfriends. 3. You are not allowed to complain about how much things cost. 4. You are not allowed to say the word "Crotch."

And so it went.

Michele and Anna were so pleased with the list, they showed it to Cannon as soon as we arrived. She thought it was hilarious and agreed with every forbidden item.

I decided that I'd be a good sport and make a game of it. I put the card in my pocket and resolved to try and not break any of the rules for the duration of the weekend. I invited them to keep score.

So, I made it through the walk around campus with no infractions. I made it through the sorority parent's formal that night. I made it through the brunch they had organized for us at the Alpha Chi Omega house the next morning. And I was still going strong, as we were taking a tour of the sorority house, where we joined in with another set of parents from Washington, D.C.

As we toured a bedroom in the sorority house, I heard the D.C. dad say to his daughter, "Why don't you ever keep your room this clean at home?" His daughter, Bethany I think, rolled her eyes and gave the D.C. dad an expression of pure venom. The girl's mother touched my wife Michele's arm and said, "My husband is always saying things that embarrass our daughter."

To which Michele replied, in a conspiratorial tone, "My husband is carrying a card with everything written on it that he's not supposed to say."

"Really?" she asked. "He's carrying a card?"

"Oh yes," Michele said proudly. "He's got it in his pocket right now."

And the funny thing is.....I did.

Tough Neighborhood

———•••———

I hope you'll forgive me if I make this short because I really need to be outside seeding, fertilizing or doing something to get my grass to grow.

You see, I live in a tough neighborhood.

Across the street I've got George, whose yard is so perfectly manicured, I secretly think he edges with a razorblade. And, I can't confirm this, but I suspect he weeds with tweezers. His Japanese maple is so pretty it looks like –well....close your eyes and think of what the perfect bonsai tree would look like and you've got a pretty good idea. Needless to say, his grass is the greenest green, and his beds are the prettiest beds on the street.

And it gets worse. To the right of George, I've got Daniel. Daniel is another dedicated do-it-yourself yard guy. I see him out there day after day tirelessly raking, watering, trimming, and pruning. He's the type guy who doesn't use a sprinkler in August, but rather enjoys watering the grass himself. And as you can imagine, his yard is picture perfect year-round.

And as if that's not bad enough, Anthony is next door and he cheats –bigtime. Every Thursday afternoon, rain or shine, a team of landscaping professionals descend onto his yard. They race around on go-behinds and zip back and forth on machines I don't even know the names of. Some punch holes in the ground, while others swoop about carrying big vacuum bags. I think the Kansas City Royals employ fewer grounds crew, and use less equipment. But the worst part is, that instead of just spreading the pine needles around willy-nilly like I do, his yard guys are so good, they can tuck and fold the pine needles in such a way to form a sharp crease that would make a party napkin proud.

For years, I've been trying to keep up with these guys and failing badly. So last year, I decided to dig in. Literally. I reseeded all my bare spots and I spread fertilizer and crabgrass killer. By April I had it looking pretty good. So good in fact that George, Mr. Razorblade Edging himself, walked across the street, stuck out his hand and said, "Congratulations on your yard. I think this is the best it's ever looked."

I beamed with pride.

Then July happened.

All my carefully cultivated grass, my little green babies that I nurtured since birth, began to dry up, turn brown, and blow away. The crabgrass came back with a vengeance, as did the clover, and my yard slowly returned to the patchy, dust bowl that it has been for years. I'm still not exactly sure what happened, but I'm pretty sure this 100 year old oak tree that covers half my front yard decided he didn't want anything growing under, living beside or photosynthesizing nearby.

So you may be wondering why I'm mentioning all of this. Well, my other neighbor, John, just tilled up his entire yard, built a decorative stone wall, and completely reseeded. The irony is that John, until now, was the only guy on my street that I felt my yard was on par with. He was my consolation. He was the only guy whose yard I could look across at and not be reminded of a Southern Living photo shoot, and now he's gone and upped his game as well.

See, I told you I live in a tough neighborhood.

Swim Meets

—•••—

Anyone who knows me, knows that I'm a bit of a softy.

I get sentimental, particularly when it involves memories of my kids when they were little.

And so it was, the other night when I was jogging past our neighborhood swimming pool.

Judging from all the cars, this was a pretty big meet.

As I got closer, I heard the mechanical sound of a voice being projected through a bull-horn followed by that electric *honnnnk* that broadcasts the beginning of each race. Coaches shouted. Parents yelled. I stopped my jog to take in the whole scene.

You see, I have three daughters who are now 25, 22 and 17 and who have long out grown summer swim meets.

My wife, Michele, and I attended many, many meets, over the years, exactly like this one, and as I stood there, I tried to think of one pleasant memory. I racked my brain for anything I enjoyed about swim meets and came up empty.

In short, I realized that I hate, no, hate isn't a strong enough word, I realized that I absolutely loathe summer swim meets, and there are few places more miserable to be on a Tuesday night in late June or early July.

I remembered one particular meet, in which my youngest daughter Anna was competing. The temperature was a steady 98, with not even the faintest puff of breeze, and if I recall correctly, the heat index was 174.

Lugging chairs, towels, bags, drinks and snacks, my shirt was thoroughly soaked before we even got situated.

We sat and baked.

We baked while the kids were warming up. We baked during the 6 and under kiddie swims. We baked through 'breaststroke' and baked though 'butterfly.' We baked through hours and hours of watching other people's kids swim lap after lap, punctuated by the only briefest moment of our own child.....or was it our child? With each girl on our team wearing nearly identical goggles, swim caps and matching bathing suits, it's virtually impossible to tell which kid is which on the starting block, and hopeless once they get in the water.

I asked Michele, "Is that her in lane three?"

"No."

"How can you tell?"

"Those aren't her knees."

"Ah."

So, I took to rooting for the swimmer who I thought might be the underdog. And when I say rooting, I mean that I sat politely in my chair and clapped appreciatively. I did not stand on the diving board and wave a towel about furiously. I did not yell "GO Sarah! GO Sarah! GO!" in a series of high-pitched, ear-splitting shrieks like the woman who sat next to us, and whose strategy, it seemed, was to scream so loudly that her daughter could hear her even while submerged underwater.

Nor did I bring one of those air horns, that are so loud and startling that grown men have been known to wet themselves.

By 9 o'clock, thankfully, the sun had gone down and the temperature had dropped by half a degree and by 10:30 we were finishing up 'freestyle.'

"So, that's it then," I said folding up my chair on this interminably long event.

"No." Michele said. "We've still got the relays."

"Is Anna in the relays?"

"Unfortunately."

And so it went.....on and on and on. On with the screaming. On with the obnoxious air horn, and on with the heat.

As I resumed my jog, I heard someone let loose with an air horn.

I can't get sentimental about swim meets. I just can't.

Desk Phone

———•••———

The other day, I read an article in the *Wall Street Journal* about how, even in this modern, smart-phone era, where over half of Americans have dumped their land-lines, the old office desk phone refuses to die.

I must admit, I've never had a good working relationship with desk phones.

Once, very young in my career, the big boss was traveling in California, or Seattle or some such faraway place. He was calling, most likely, from his hotel room or from a pay phone, as those were really the only options back then. Anyway, I was at my desk, when I answered the call. We spoke for a bit about business stuff. I answered all of his questions.....so far so good, right?

The trouble started when he asked me to transfer him to Janet, our office man-ager. Let me just say that transferring calls has never been my strong suit. In fact, I'm terrible at it. No, I'm worse than terrible, I think I am genetically incapable of operating a large multi-button desk phone properly. I can never seem to recall which button to press first. Do you put the caller on hold first, then hit the exten-sion or is it the other way 'round? I honestly don't know. And I never did figure it out. On this occasion, I said into the receiver, "Hold on I'll transfer you to Janet....." but then I immediately and completely inadvertently hung up on him. My intention was to put him on hold while I tried to figure out how to transfer a call, but somehow, I killed the call instead. He called back. Again I said, "Hang on....I'll switch you over...." whereupon, I proceeded to......yes.....hang up on him again. Hanging up on the boss once is forgivable. Twice is annoying, but hopefully understandable, but after the third time, I'm certain he was thinking to himself, "Why did I hire this imbecile?"

So, ever since I read the article, I've been noticing desk phones. Sure enough, they are still around. On Friday, I had an appointment at Sherrill Furniture in Hickory and, I'm not kidding here, the receptionist's desk phone with so many extensions it stretched a full 3 feet across the desk. It must have held 500 different buttons. The receptionist was pressing buttons and transferring calls like mad when I approached. Missiles have been launched from less elaborate command centers.

In November of last year, I took a new job. New company, new office, new computer and yes, I got a new office desk phone. A week or two into the job I got swamped and needed all the space, so I moved the desk phone to the floor. And that's where it has sat ever since. But don't worry, in the full year since I've worked here the land line has rung only twice. Seriously. Twice. And in each case, I had to root around on the floor to pick up the receiver, only to discover it was a telemarketer.

Which in my case, is probably a good thing. I figure the fewer calls I get on the office desk phone, the less likely I am to inadvertently hang up on someone.

And for the record, I don't think my old boss' call ever got connected to Janet the office manager.

Grandpa Names Galore

——•••——

I've been asking around about grandfather names, after a close friend of mine, Thom Stout, became a grandfather last month. I was hoping I could offer him some cool, hip and hopefully fitting suggestions.

My first call was to Bill Colonna. Bill is one of the most sensible guys I know, so I guess I wasn't surprised when he said his grandchildren call him Grandpa. I made several more calls and discovered a Pap-Paw and a Papa until I realized that I could reach a lot more people if I posted on my Facebook page.

I asked for any interesting or unusual names that kids call their grandfather and within just a few minutes, my in-box began filling up.

The first was from a friend and former co-worker, Lisa Martin, who wrote that her father, John Martin, a textile executive and mill owner, goes by Bauble because her niece couldn't pronounce Pa Pa.

The next was Kelly Johnson who wrote me that she called her Grandfather: Grandpa Goopy. She explained that Grandpa Goopy's real name was Ken Owen and he was the vice president of Casard Furniture in High Point.

Already, this was getting interesting, plus I like the idea of these prominent men, both executives, going by such silly monikers as Bauble and Goopy. I couldn't wait to see if anyone else would send me a message.

As the evening wore on, Jennifer Linnell said her child called her father BobBob.

Brian Hatley shared that when he was little, he called his grandfather Buddy, only to learn later that his real name was actually Buddy.

Elizabeth Sheffield, of High Point, wrote to say that her father, Richard Wood, former VP of George T. Wood & Sons and later an advisor with Wells Fargo, and Chairman of The City Project in High Point, is called Foxy by his grandchildren.

Elizabeth said Richard claimed that he used this name for his own Grandfather, but she's never seen any proof of this and she suspects he just likes the name Foxy.

All night long, and into the next day, my phone chirped, tweeted, dinged, and buzzed with more and more messages.

Karen Austin shared that her kids called her father Toots. I love the name Toots, I think because it sounds like the bassist in a reggae band.

Sterling Cannon shared that his grandfather went by the name Bullet because at NC State, he mixed a drink that was as lethal as a bullet.

Paige Tyde said her oldest called her father-in-law Grandmadaddy. Apparently, this arose from the prompt "give your hugs to Grandma and Grandaddy, whereupon her daughter shortened this to Grandma and Grandmadaddy.

I've never met Paige's father-in-law, but I imagined a distinguished, gray haired gentleman with a dignified air about him going by the name Grandmadddy?

This was getting seriously hilarious, and they just kept getting better and better.

Trevor Whitson shared that his Father is called Popeye by all his Grand-darlings.

I also learned that when the kids are allowed to choose the name –or worse pronounce the name for the first time-you can often get some doozies.

I heard about Ha Ha, Two Pops, Papa Bear, Gang Gang, Papoo and Old Dad. My Facebook friends shared stories about Pawkie, DooDaddy, Fa, Two Paws, and Piney.

I imagined being at a social gathering and introducing all these guys to one another. "GrandpaGoopy meet Doo Daddy. Goopy Doo. Doo Goopy." Or "HaHa come over here, I want you to meet Grandmadaddy."

In truth, this whole exercise didn't really help me in my quest to find a name for my friend. Incidentally, he choose the name Poppie without any help from me- but it did help me not feel so bad about the nickname I called my own grandfather. I called him Mean Mean for the first few years of my life.

I mean honestly, Mean Mean doesn't sound so weird in this crowd.....does it?

Get Your Ass to the Hospital

————•••————

So how does a guy like me, a guy who runs marathons, and a guy who exercises like a fiend- have a bloody heart attack at age 49?

It happened like this: on the Tuesday before Christmas, I attended a boot-camp style work-out. I've been training with the guys at F-3 for about 4 months now, anyway, after this particular workout, I started feeling really weird. Like stomach flu weird, but not exactly. On the drive home I broke into a cold clammy sweat. I felt nauseous, and there was a tightness in my chest. Keep in mind that I'd just done crazy reps of pull-ups, push-ups and dips for crying out-loud, so I was expecting to feel tightness in the chest.

At home, I told my wife Michele how I felt.

I was thinking dehydration. Michele was thinking hospital.

I don't know what exactly I expected a heart attack to feel like, but this didn't seem that bad. There was no elephant on my chest like I'd always heard about, plus I just couldn't wrap my mind around the fact that I might be having a heart attack. It seemed inconceivable. So, my plan was to try some juice and give it a little time to see if the feeling would pass. Michele's plan was to get my dad on the phone. Dad had a heart attack in 2015, and Michele knew if anyone could bully me into going, it would be Dad.

On the phone, I told Dad that I thought I was just dehydrated, but he was having none of it. He yelled into the phone: "Get your ass to the hospital.....immediately!"

At the hospital, they tested my troponin levels and determined I was having a cardiac event, but they didn't know how bad it was until the cardiologist ran the scope into my heart and discovered a large clot (embolism) in the coronary artery known as the "widow maker" (the left anterior descending coronary artery). From the name, you can surmise this is among the very worst places possible to have a clot. This is the same kind of heart attack from which newsman Tim Russert of NBC died a few years back.

For treatment, I was hooked up to 4 IVs and was given blood-thinners and clot dissolving medicines and was ordered to stay immobile for two days.

On day three, the cardiologists went into my heart through my leg. As it turns out, instead of shrinking, the clot had grown to a 99% blockage.

In what I'm told is a delicate procedure, and after two tries, they removed the clot with some sort of suction device and inserted a stent in its place.

Amazingly, I was up and walking by 11:00 pm and doing laps around the cardiac ward at 8:00 AM the next morning.

So now, I'm better. Fixed. And marveling at everything that's taken place. For those of you who know me, you know that I have a strong faith -and I certainly needed it during all this trauma. I was at total peace with God whatever the outcome.

I'd also like to thank Dr. Woody in ER, and Cardiolosts -Dr. Chiu and Dr. Cheek -as well as the whole Cardiac Team at High Point Regional. The nurses, lab techs, everyone. Even the phlebotomists who woke me up at 3:00 AM to draw yet more blood.....each of you had a part in saving my life and I will forever be profoundly grateful.

It was Dr. Woody who told me afterward, that the type heart attack I had is "usually fatal."

I'd also like to thank God that I have the best wife on the planet, as well as my three daughters, who were just awesome during this whole ordeal. Also, my mom and stepfather who rushed over as soon as they heard the news, my in-laws, and grandmother, as well as everyone who said a prayer for us during this 4-day roller coaster ride.

In closing, my best advice to anyone is: If you think you even kinda, sorta, maybe, perhaps, possibly, think you may be having any of the symptoms of a heart attack.....GET YOUR ASS TO THE HOSPITAL....IMMEDIATELY.

I'm sure glad I did.

Time for the Readers

—•••—

I need you to help me keep this a secret.

I've just purchased a pair of reading glasses, and I don't know how I feel about the whole world knowing I've reached that particular stage in my life.

Up until just a week ago, I had never given reading glasses –or any kind of glasses for that matter– even a passing thought.

If pressed, I might have said something like, OK, sure, but not until I'm older. Much older.

This would still be true if not for a recent trip to the drugstore.

My wife was attempting to sign my daughter up for a flu shot. This involved filling out 12 different color-coded forms, and showing of several different types of identification; I think maybe even an arm wrestling match with the assistant pharmacist, before she was told that we did not qualify and we would be expected to fork over a large sum of money if we wanted the flu shot.

As my wife was handling all that, I was productively doodling around in the store. I checked out the Dr. Scholl's foot display and walked aimlessly down the aisles several times, until, being now totally bored, I eventually wandered over to a display of reading glasses for sale.

Having nothing else at the moment to occupy my attention, I slipped on a pair of 1.25's.

As I hinted earlier, I am one of those folks who has always had exceptional eyesight. Normally, when I try on glasses, like my wife's spectacles for example, I see a severely distorted world. Imagine holding the mouth of a Coke bottle up to your eye and attempting to look through it lengthwise like a telescope. That is my experience with nearly every pair of prescription glasses I've ever tried on.

So, as you can imagine, I was expecting the Coke-bottle-telescope view of the world when –HOLY COW- I slipped on the pair of drugstore reading glasses.

What I saw before me was simply amazing!

Incredibly, I noticed how clear and well-defined everything looked. It was as if the small print on the display was suddenly larger, clearer and supernaturally somehow closer to my face.

Everything was so clear.

As I studied the view some more, I noticed printed letters like "rn" didn't look like "m" as they did before.

I was stunned.

These are magic glasses.

I stood there for a few more minutes simply marveling.

Around the corner, I grabbed a bottle of cold medicine off the shelf. I looked at the microscopic printing on the side label. With these reading glasses, it was like the letters were being mysteriously lifted toward my face.

I slid the glasses off and attempted to read the same fine print with my naked eyes.

I would like for the record to state: I could still make out the print, but it wasn't as easy, as clear, or as much fun.

Since that day, I haven't stopped thinking about how well those reading glasses worked or how much more I would enjoy reading the newspaper in the morning if I didn't have to strain.

How much easier I could see text messages on my iPhone?

My only hesitation is that –old men wear reading glasses and I am definitely not an old man yet……but I bought the glasses anyway.

Youngest Daughter Drives

———•••———

My youngest daughter, Anna, just got her driver's license, and I have to admit, that for just a minute or two, I was tempted to write one of those syrupy 'where did the time go?' pieces. You know the kind. A mushy sentimental column filled with all the requisite clichés like 'Time flies' and 'kids grow-up sooo fast.' But truth is, I can't bring myself to do it. I'm finding it hard to write a mushy column when I don't feel even the slightest bit mushy. I know. I know. This is odd for me right? I mean, I'm the kind of guy who cries at coffee commercials, so this is really strange for me not to feel even the least bit melancholy at such a momentous milestone. But with Anna's new driver's license, I now have all three of my children able to get themselves from one place to another, and I must confess, I don't feel even the slightest bit sad, mostly because it's so incredibly wonderful!

The same day Anna got her license, she drove herself to swim practice.

Did you get that? She drove herself to swim practice. Not me. Not my wife. Anna drove herself.

For 24 years, my wife and I have been carting these children from one place to another, and now it's finally over. Year after…year after….year of driving to soccer practice, volleyball games, rock climbing competitions, swim meets, sleep overs, doctor's appointments. Over and over. Back and forth; back and forth.

Do you know how many carpool lines I've sat in? Do you know how many carpool lines my wife has sat in?

It's staggering the amount of transportation children require. It's like a full-time job that nobody tells you about when you become a parent.

I recall a few hellish years when two out of three of our kids attended a magnet school in Greensboro. Either Michele or I would drive from High Point to Greensboro and back…. twice… each day for the entire 185 days of the school calendar. That's 370 trips to Greensboro and 370 trips back. And joy upon joy, on days when there was an open house or special program in the evening, we'd all hop back into the car and drive to Greensboro and back for a third time that day.

Truck drivers felt sorry for us: we were behind the wheel so much.

And on the weekends, we'd often have three activities, with three separate children, all on the same day.

Michele and I would get the calendar out the night before to strategize. "You go to volleyball game and gymnastics practice and I'll drive to soccer, rock climbing and Sara's birthday party." And just when we thought we'd gotten it all organized, invariably one of our children would announce, "I need to go to Courtney's house on Saturday to work on a school project." And we'd have to start all over….

And this went on for years. As I mentioned, our oldest is 24, so we've been at it at least that long.

But that's all over now thanks to a little piece of laminated plastic issued by the great state of North Carolina.

The other night, Michele said, "Oh, no. We're out of eggs."

I was thinking of how dark and cold and rainy it was, and how much I was dreading driving to the grocery store to buy eggs.

But, out of the blue, Anna piped up, and said, "I can drive and get some."

Driving is so new and novel for Anna that she leaps at any chance to get behind the wheel, even if it's eggs in the rain.

I wept from delight as she got out her keys.

As she drove off I mouthed a silent prayer, "God bless Anna. God bless the Driver's License Bureau and God bless everyone at the DMV" I said.

This driving thing just keeps getting better and better.

These Balding and Graying Guys
Are My Classmates

———•••———

Yes, I turned the big five-zero this summer, but it's not my age that I'm bothered by.

What does bother me, and quite a lot if you want to know the truth –and I know this sounds obvious on the surface– is that all my friends have turned 50 this year as well.

For me, this is way, way, way harder to accept. Impossible, if you want to know the truth.

I'm sorry, but Thom Stout is not a 50 year old man. Nor will he ever be. Scott Smith, no way. Not in my mind at least. Same goes for Moon, Brooke, Randy, Quin, Richard, Jay, David, Todd, Brian, David, Bill and Neil. Jim Stroupe is definitely not 50 years old. But alas, he is. And they all are. Stout is actually a grandfather, but I can't spend time thinking about that because it POSITIVELY FREAKS ME OUT. And yet, here they are. All these balding, graying, guys with bulging-waistlines....these guys ARE my classmates, and they look like, for all the world to see...like....well....50 year old men.

It just doesn't seem possible, and that's what I'm having the hardest time wrapping my mind around.

But the biggest question I have is, and also the most dumbfounding question of all: what happened to all this time? We are talking huge amounts of time that have passed by since high school in what seems like nanoseconds.

Honestly? How did all my friends get to this point in life so quickly? The best answer I have is that time has been speeding up. That's right. Time has actually been passing by more and more quickly each year since about 1973, and I think I can prove it.

My proof is that when I was younger, time was different. Far different. As an example, growing up, I once spent 3 weeks waiting for my mother to get her hair done.

When I was young, the drive to Myrtle Beach took 17 ½ hours, and the month of December –don't even get me started on the month of December– the timespan between when the "Wish Book Catalog" arrived in the mailbox, until Christmas itself, lasted for entire decades.

One Tuesday afternoon, I spent an entire semester waiting for Sr. Sanchez's fourth period Spanish class to end.

You see, in those days, and for me at least, everything ran on childhood time. Childhood time lasts so long that fossils can form. (If you don't believe me check under my desk in Mrs. Phillips' 5th grade classroom.)

Then after childhood time was over, the world ran on college time. College time is measured in beer, not hours.

Next was actual time, and by actual time, I mean father-of-three time.

Father-of-three time is the fastest time of all...... It's spectacularly fast. In father-of-three time, children reach puberty in about the same time period it takes to chew a piece of gum. In father-of-three time, one moment my oldest is in diapers, then a stick-legged little girl kicking a soccer ball around in the backyard, then in a blink, law school.

So, what's next? Empty-nest time? I'm honestly worried that if time keeps accelerating at this same pace, I'll be in some assisted living facility, drooling into a bib, before I'm finished writing this column.

But at least all my friends will be there too. But I don't know if that will be comforting or not to tell the truth.

I can't bear the thought of all them being that old.

But of course, so will I.

Launching Produce

———•••———

One hot, long and boring summer when I was about 14 or so, Jay Hughes and I built a tennis ball cannon. Three tennis ball cans duct taped together formed the barrel of this home-made bazooka-like device. Jay poured lighter fluid into an opening at the bottom, while I stuffed a ball down the barrel and aimed. Our cannon could shoot a tennis ball several hundred feet into the air. And of course, after a few skyward test shots, we targeted more terrestrial objects: Mrs. Grubb's garage, Mr. Womble's side house, Mrs. Walls' trash can, and if I recall correctly, even a passing Buick got pelted by our launcher.

Up to that point in my life, bombing the neighborhood with tennis balls was some of the best fun I'd ever had.

What brought this to mind is that, on impulse, my wife ordered a three-man sling shot on-line –called "The Beast." She showed it to us at dinner the other night and asked with a smile, "Want to try it out?"

"What will we use for ammo?" I asked.

"Look in the fridge," she said. "I think we've got an orange and maybe some lemons."

The street was dark as Michele and I held the handles while our daughter loaded a lemon into the pouch, pulled back the rubber straps about 6 or 7 feet, and let her rip.

Our goal was to see how far we could launch stuff down our deserted street. Unfortunately, we watched our third shot -a speeding lemon- explode as it made impact against my neighbor's mailbox. It hit with a hard whammthhh sound.

Suddenly, I was 14 again. Should we run for it? For the briefest moment, I had a flashback of Mrs. Grubb calling the cops. Then I got hold of myself. I can't run. I own the house I'm standing in front of. In fact, I have a mortgage to prove it.

The next day I saw my neighbor, Charles, out in his yard. I walked over. Trying to muster all the dignity and credibility a 51-year-old balding man who just spent the previous evening launching citrus fruit down the street can muster, I said, "Hi Charles. We were testing out our new three-man sling shot last night after dinner, and we accidentally shot your mailbox with a lemon. It hit really hard. In fact, the lemon exploded on impact into about a million pieces."

Charles smiled.

But do you want to know what the weirdest part is? I live across the street from where Jay Hughes lived when we were growing up. And on the night of the mailbox shooting, I was standing on almost exactly the same spot that Jay and I once bombarded the block with tennis balls of terror some 37 years ago.

And I have to say, it was fun then, and it's fun now.

Aim a Little Higher

———•••———

Our youngest child, my sweet little baby Peppy-Pepperoni, is graduating from high school this spring, and if you are expecting another sweet, sentimental-where-has-the-time-gone sort of piece…well…..you can forget it.

No tears for me -well at least not yet- because I'm so excited it's hard for me to keep my mouth shut. Darn near impossible, if you want to know the truth.

You see, Anna, (her actual name) is the third of my children that I have tried desperately to coax, cajole, persuade, sweet-talk, interest, or otherwise convince to attend, the single greatest institute of higher learning on the planet – which also happens to be located in the single greatest college town in the universe.

Now I understand that in our wonderful state of North Carolina, we have lots of excellent state-supported universities from which to choose. UNC Chapel Hill, UNC-Wilmington, East Carolina, NC A&T and NC State immediately come to mind, and these are all outstanding schools to be sure. But what's got me so excited is that Anna has set her sights a little higher. Yes. That's right, like her father, Anna will become a Mountaineer in the fall when she begins classes at Appalachian State University. (Just typing those words sent goose bumps down my arms.)

My wife has accused me of brain-washing Anna from an early age.

No dear. Those were just fun ski trips, and while Kidd Brewer Stadium isn't exactly on the way to Beech Mountain, what's the harm in driving past? Or for that matter, is there any danger in stopping in for a burger at the T'App Room while we are passing through?

I can honestly say I've never had her watch the last 5 minutes of the 2007 ASU vs. #3 Michigan game. I was holding that back as my ace card. (I just got more goose bumps…..in fact…..hold on. I just realized I haven't watched it in a few months and I feel a hankering coming on. Ok. I'm back. Don't worry! And all is well. Corey Lynch still blocks the field goal attempt and ASU still wins the single biggest upset in college football history.)

So, on Wednesday, my wife Michele, Anna and I drove to Boone for accepted students' day. The car practically drove itself. Like a horse that knows its way back to the barn, my Jeep seemed to enjoy the steep climb up Highway 421 into the High Country.

The hardest part, as I mentioned, was me keeping my mouth shut. As we toured the campus with our student guide, it was extremely hard for me not to chime in a few select remarks.

Michele coached me before the trip. "This is about Anna and not about you. She needs to make her own memories up here and not be bombarded by yours."

I agreed. And I tried really hard. I did. And for the most part I succeeded, although I couldn't restrain myself when I saw the new food court that replaced the Bavarian Inn or B.I. for short. "They used to serve the nastiest food here you can imagine. The chicken sandwiches tasted just like the corn dogs and somehow the burgers also tasted just like the corn dogs. I don't know how they did it, but somehow everything they served tasted exactly the same. It was horrible," I said with a big grin. "And the food spun around on this giant revolving rotisserie thing we called the wheel of death."

My wife and daughter gave me a look of astonishment. Astonished that anyone could be so blissfully nostalgic about such apparently bad food.

In all, I managed to keep my mouth closed most of the time. I'd give myself a C-.

But I'll give Anna an A+ for choosing the right school.

Dad's New Tesla

——•••——

I want to give fair warning to anyone on the streets of Greensboro who may drive a Porsche, a Corvette, Mustang, or one of those super-fast Dodge hemi things: my father is gunning for you.

The other day I was on the cell phone with him during one such roadway encounter.

"Hold on. Hold on. I'm just pulling up at a red light next to a Corvette convertible," Dad was narrating into the speakerphone. " Ohhhh.....I wish you could see this guy. He thinks he's mister cool. Top down. Shades on. I'm trying to get his attention now. I'm giving him the 'let's go' signal. Hold on.......Ok.....He just pointed forward. Looks like we've got ourselves a race."

Normally dad's voice is gruff and commanding, but today there was glee in it. Joyful glee.

"Does he recognize what you are driving?" I asked.

"Don't think so."

Which is not surprising. Dad's new Tesla Model 3 at first glance, looks like a Toyota, or a Kia but definitely NOT like a lightning fast hotrod. Think: standard issue, four door, family sedan and you've got a pretty good idea.

"Green light," Dad hooted. "We're off!"

"Did you get him?" I asked after a few seconds.

"Oh heck yeah. I let off the gas at 70 and he was 4 car lengths behind me. Ha!" he shouted. "Mr. Corvette is back there scratching his head and wondering what the hell just happened."

Another odd thing is that Dad's Tesla doesn't make any noise to speak of. So, when he's out there eating Corvettes for lunch, there is no sound, no roar of the engine, no smoke pouring out of the back, no burning rubber. In fact, the dual electric motors are golf-cart-quiet as it accelerates to heart-lurching-up-into-your-throat fast.

According to the website, the Telsa Model 3 has a top speed of 162 MPH, but the most impressive feature is that it accelerates from 0 to 60 in 3.2 seconds.

For comparison, I did a little poking around on-line and I've listed the 0-60 stats of some muscle cars below and the Tesla beats all of them:

> 2019 Corvette Stingray – 3.7 seconds
> 2019 Dodge Charger SRT Hellcat – 3.6 seconds
> 2019 Ford Mustang GT Fastback – 4.2 seconds
> 2019 Porsche 911 Carrera -4.2 seconds

About a month after Dad bought the car, my wife Michele said, "I don't think I've ever seen your father this happy."

And I have to agree. He really is like a teenager with a new hot rod. Or, check that, he as happy as a teenager with a new hot rod, back when teenagers cared about such things.

So, a word to the wise: if a non-descript, 4 door sedan pulls up beside you, and the driver has a twinkle in his eye as he motions for you to race….you are welcome to give it a shot….but my money is on the Tesla.

Forgetfulness

—●●●—

Now that I am getting older, I've discovered three things. I can watch a movie without being able to say for certain if I've seen it before. I can fall asleep in almost any position, and I can't remember the third thing.

That is the problem with getting older —you can't remember anything. And for me, it's getting worse. Just the other day I called my wife to ask: "Why am I at Food Lion?"

"I gave you a list."

"Oh yes. Right. Do you know where I put the list?"

Here lately, I often find myself standing in the laundry room, my closet, or some other part the of the house, staring up, scratching my head, lips pursed in a thoughtful manner, and thinking: Why did I come in here? Was I looking for my pants. No. It seems I am already wearing pants. Shoes. No. At which point, I will go back downstairs, wander from room to room in search of something, anything, that will remind me of why I went there in the first place. Usually, in the course of my wandering about, I will find something else that needs looking into -like a light bulb that has burned out, say, which will cause me to wander back into the laundry room only to stare up, with no idea as to why I am there.

So, with this in mind, I want to share with you an incident that happened yesterday. My office is on the 9th floor in the Market Square Tower in High Point. I arrived, and as usual, I used my key to unlock the office door, just like I've done hundreds of times before. But yesterday, upon returning from lunch, I discovered my key wouldn't fit. I turned it upside down, back and forth, side to side and I could not, for the life of me, get the cussed thing to fit into the lock.

Knowing how forgetful I can be, I checked to see if this was the correct key. It was. And that I was on the correct floor. I was. And I know how stupid this must sound, but I even read, and re-read the sign above the door to make certain I wasn't trying to Watergate into someone else's office by mistake.

As I stood there, I noticed three persons who work in the office down the hall walking past in the corridor. They are my competitors. I waved, swallowed hard, tried to act nonchalant as I did my best to strike an I-certainly-have-a-very-good-reason-for-standing-in-the-hallway-outside-my-office-like-this type pose.

I felt ridiculous.

I tried to think of other possibilities? Had I been fired? Is Candid Camera filming this?

I swallowed hard, took the elevator down to security, and begged to be let into my own office.

Later in the day the property manager called. "I'm sorry Mac. We changed the lock on your door, but we failed to notify you."

Normally, something like this would make me furious, but I was honestly so relieved that I wasn't completely losing my marbles, I found I couldn't get angry at all.

And I'll let you know what the moral of this story is, as soon as I can remember it myself.

A Megalodon for Ma

—•••—

Every summer, and for as far back into my childhood as I can remember, my grandmother and I spent hour upon hour scouring the beach for shark's teeth.

Just the two of us, hunched over, right along the water's edge, we searched.

I found hundreds. Ma found thousands —by virtue of the fact that she and my grandfather owned a house at the beach and Ma looked nearly every day in the summer.

Any time I stooped to pick something up, Ma would ask, "You get one?"

Some of our favorites were the thick-rooted tiger shark and long dagger-like sand shark's teeth, as well as Hemipristis' teeth, which are serrated, hooked and look wickedly dangerous. We also found teeth from great whites, hammerheads, bull sharks, lemon, six gills and prehistoric makos.

Other times, I would pick up a fooler. (As you probably guessed, a fooler is a bit of shell or rock that resembles the shape of a shark's tooth.)

But there is one type of shark's tooth that Ma and I always dreamed of finding: that of the extinct Carcharodon Megalodon — the Megalodon, or meg.

Not only is it a whopper of a tooth — some Megalodon teeth are as large as your hand — but they are also quite rare. So rare, that many beachcombers, like Ma and me, can go a whole lifetime and never find one. (Ma has come across several meg teeth in her lifetime, but these were found in gift shops or bought from other collectors.)

So, you can imagine my excitement when, a few weeks ago, three friends from High Point — Eric Hill, Ray Soltis and Joe Fisher — invited me to join them on a scuba diving trip specifically to find Megalodons off the North Carolina coast.

"I'm in," I said in a rush of excitement, forgetting that I hadn't been scuba diving in more than 20 years.

After a refresher class, a Nitrox class and an advanced certification class, I was ready to dive for Megs.

We met the boat's captain, Chris Slog, and mate, Brett Garner, of Wrightsville Beach Diving at the boat dock at 6:30 a.m. After an hour and a half boat ride out into the blue Atlantic, Captain Chris dropped an anchor buoy and told us to get our gear on.

Thirty seven miles off Wrightsville Beach and in 97 feet of water, I had only been at bottom for a few seconds, when I noticed something slightly triangular among the sand and rubble. Was this a fooler? I thought back to all those days of walking along the beach with my grandmother, and how — over many years — I learned to recognize the distinctive shape of a shark's tooth.

My heart pounded. I swallowed hard as I reached to pick it up.

Jackpot. It was a Megalodon tooth.

My dive buddy Eric gave me a thumbs up.

And, as it turns out, this was the first of eight enormous Megalodon teeth I would find that day.

The only thing I could think about the whole time I was under water was: I can't wait to show this to Ma.

Nothing is Normal

———•••———

Imagine two time travelers stepping into a futuristic time machine. The first spins the dial, looks to the other and says, "What about 2020?" The second says, "No! No! No! That's a terrible year! Pick any other year but that one."

No other way around it -for me, and I'm sure for most of you too- this is perhaps the weirdest, and most unsettling time we've ever lived through.

Also, rest assured, I will not harp on about the obvious. We all know there has been a run on toilet paper. March Madness, Furniture Market, Easter Services, my daughter's freshman year of college, and nearly everything else under the sun, has been cancelled, postponed, moved online or stopped.....except apparently, telemarketers.

I don't know anyone who isn't worried. Worried about our parents and grandparents. Worried about our jobs and livelihoods.

There is one thing I'd like to share about grocery shopping in this new normal we suddenly find ourselves in.

Under normal circumstances, I am a terrible grocery shopper – and by normal circumstances, I mean, anytime in the past when I didn't feel the need to wear a mask and have hand sanitizer at the ready, when I venture out.

A trip to Publix starts off easily enough. My wife, Michele, will say, "Oh, and can you also pick up a can of tomatoes while you are there?"

"Happy to!" I reply with a smile.

Dutifully, I locate the canned tomato section and stand there open-mouthed and bewildered. Crushed. Diced. Paste. Pureed. Whole. Stewed. Stewed with Garlic. Diced with No Salt. Crushed with No Salt. And this is only the beginning. Of each of the varieties, there are four or five different manufacturers and at least 4 different sizes, not to mention there is also a store brand of all the above.

Once, by pure luck, I actually bought the correct kind of canned tomatoes, only to be admonished because the can was dented.

But perhaps the worst section in the store is the Orange Juice aisle. And as I've mentioned in a column from years ago, there is: Original-No Pulp, Original Home-Style -Low Pulp, High Pulp with Added Calcium with Vitamin D, Low Acid -No Pulp, Light and Healthy with Half the Calories, Healthy Heart, Immunity Defense No Pulp, Country Style and Donald Duck.

It's bewildering, but the coronavirus has changed all that.

Suddenly, I'm a rock star of grocery shopping. Thanks to the pandemic, I now make wise, brilliant and exceptional choices. Store brand, off-brand, giant-size, trial-size or the odd variety with some sort of weird and unexpected ingredient like Jalapenos added, is now perfectly acceptable and appreciated.

Any level of pulp is applauded. In fact, I'm batting a thousand.

My wife is now thrilled with whatever I bring home, and more importantly, she's just happy I made it back from the store alive, and if I also have a bag of potatoes, or a can of any kind of canned tomatoes at all, so much the better.

Room at Home

———•••———

Despite an aging roof, and a cracked driveway, our house has treated us well.

We've gone from Pampers to Pandemic at this same address.

The Lanes -there were only three of us at the time- moved in when my oldest was 3 and now she's 27 and living on her own.

One by one our daughters have each flown the coop. Anna, our youngest, moved into her freshman dorm room at Appalachian State back in August, leaving Michele and I alone for the first time.

The adjustment was hard.

Hard for me, and hard for Michele.

Michele moped. I sulked.

One morning, I stopped at the top of the stairs and just cried. I got choked up at the memory of all those by-gone Christmas mornings –when I stood in this same spot as we got ready to go downstairs to see if Santa Claus had come.

After being parents for so long, and suddenly finding ourselves with no kids around, we honestly didn't know what to do with ourselves.

Evenings, after work, we'd look at each other blankly.

"Do you want to cook something or get take out?"

And, most nights, you know what we did? Neither. Sadly, there were many evenings, where we were both completely satisfied to dine on popcorn while we watched NetFlix.

Why bother? It's hard to get motivated to cook when there is no group to cook for.

And even though our house isn't huge, it felt cavernous with room after empty room. With just me and my 115 lb wife -I quickly discovered she and I don't take up much space.

If I snored, Michele could have her pick of any one of the three spare bedrooms vacated by our grown children.

For about a week or two, we considered turning one of the empty bedrooms into an office or an exercise room or a craft-room, but we didn't discuss it very seriously.

I read somewhere that one of the biggest fears a new college student has, is that they won't have a room at home to return to…..the article said something about how they want to keep a beachhead in their former life.

And now, in hindsight, I am profoundly glad we didn't make any changes. Because, as I'm sure you know, on March 11th, as part of the Covid-19 Shut Down, the UNC system cancelled all in-person classes, and closed all the dormitories. This forced Anna home. Her older sister Cannon, who is attending her second year of grad-school, made the choice to come home as well, rather than be stuck alone in a one bedroom apartment in Chapel Hill for the duration of the pandemic.

So now, our nest isn't empty anymore, and I love it.

There's no moping around from room to room. There's no quibbling about what not to eat for dinner.

We cook. The fact that there is dinner pleases me, but not nearly as much as having our nest not be empty.

I guess the point of this is: there is always room at home.

Bad Year, Good Grass

———•••———

My daughter's car was broken into over the weekend. We called the police. The officer arrived. You know the drill.

The policeman and I met in the middle of my front lawn and spoke for a bit. Very routine.

Then, something extraordinary happened. And when I say extraordinary, I mean just that. Something so wonderful, that I'm still smiling at the memory and this was days ago. The policeman suddenly stopped writing in his little notebook, looked down, then he gazed out across my yard and said, "You sure do have some pretty grass."

"Uhhhhhh. Thank you," was the best I could muster, because I was so absolutely flabbergasted by the compliment.

To let you know how deep this goes with me, you need to know the depth of my struggles in the whole area of lawn care and how I positively ache for decent grass.

I've lived at this same address for 24 years. And in those years, I've coveted my neighbor Daniel's lawn as it stretches beautifully from curb to driveway without any card-table size bare patches like in my own. And how year after painful year, you need to know how I've looked across the street at my neighbor George's perfectly green, weed-less yard and felt even more hopeless about how my pathetic plot looks in comparison.

I've spent more money fighting crabgrass than I spent raising my third child. Well, the formative years anyhow. College is more expensive than crabgrass.

And how most years, I would have settled for not even decent, but passable. No, that's not exactly right either, most years I would have gladly settled for anything green and not-dirt.

But as I looked across my yard on this particular morning, I noticed the same thing the policeman noticed. My grass was actually pretty, and it did look nice. Full, green and lush, like a lawn should be.

And to be honest, I'm not sure exactly how it happened. I reseeded in October, same as every year. I fertilized. I applied crabgrass preventer in late February, same as in years before. So then, as I stood there with the police officer, I thought, how ironic. That 2020 has been the single most unsettling and fretful year....the year that everything has seemingly gone wrong, and in the year that everyone I know is the most scared, frightened, and nervous. So ironically, in the one year where everything seems to go badly, oddly, my lawn is fabulous. It is the best it's ever looked, by far. It's July and there is actual grass and not dirt.

Even the clover is politely staying in the back yard, where no one can really see.

Then the policeman asked, "Do you do it yourself or do you have a service?"

"I do it myself," I stammered. "But usually it's a disaster. I think maybe it's all the rain we've been having."

He nodded appreciatively and went back to taking notes about the break-in.

And I'm still smiling about it. The yard thing runs deep with me.

Tag Lines

————•••————

Years ago, my editor encouraged me to tailor my tag line to match the piece. I've included some of my favorites:

When Mac Lane is not scraping day old birthday cake into the trash can, he can be reached at maclane@northstate.net

Mac Lane is growing old in High Point, NC. He can be reached at maclane@northstate.net

When Mac Lane isn't getting exited around large tubs of salad dressing, he can be reached at maclane@northstate.net

If you have had success against crabgrass, please contact Mac at maclane@northstate.net He is really desperate.

Mac Lane lives in High Point and is pretty sure he works in the Home Furnishings Industry. He can be contacted at: maclane@northstate.net

Mac Lane lives in High Point, is the father of three, and when he's not dressing up his cats, he can be reached at maclane@northstate.net

Mac Lane lives in High Point, is the father of three and works in the home furnishings industry -and when he's not bombing his neighbor's property with flying produce- he can be reached at maclane@northstate.net

Mac Lane lives in High Point, works in the Home Furnishings Industry and when he's not struggling with lawn care he can be reached at maclane@northstate.net

When he's not contemplating running naked through the streets of High Point, Mac Lane is the father of three, works in the Home Furnishings Industry, and can be contacted at maclane@northstate.net

When he isn't humming Grease songs, High Point resident, Mac Lane works in sales in the Home Furnishings Industry. He can be contacted at maclane@ northstate.net

Mac Lane can be reached at maclane@northstate.net And he's still looking for unusual or interesting names children call the grandparents. If you'd like to share, please send him an email.

When Mac Lane isn't desperately trying to figure out what's going on within his own household, he can be reached at maclane@northstate.net

If you have any tips on how to avoid a similar gardening disaster next year, you can email Mac at maclane@northstate.net

When he's not dreaming of angry-knife-wielding caterers chasing him through dark alleys demanding he fork over thousands of dollars for crab puffs and bacon-wrapped shrimp on those little bamboo skewers, Mac Lane can be reached at maclane@northstate.net

Okay. Really not kidding about the crabgrass thing. If you can help, please contact Mac at maclane@northstate.net